The Economics of
FORCED LABOR
The Soviet Gulag

T0148741

The Economics of
FORCED LABOR
The Soviet Gulag

EDITED BY

Paul R. Gregory
and Valery Lazarev

FOREWORD BY

Robert Conquest

HOOVER INSTITUTION PRESS
Stanford University   Stanford, California

www.hoover.org

Hoover Institution Press Publication No. 518

First printing 2003
09 08 07 06 05 04 03   9 8 7 6 5 4 3 2 1

Manufactured in the United States of America

The paper used in this publication meets the minimum requirements
of American National Standard for Information Sciences—Permanence
of Paper for Printed Library Materials, ANSI Z39.48-1984. ⊚

Library of Congress Cataloging-in-Publication Data

The economics of forced labor : the Soviet Gulag / edited by Paul R. Gregory
and Valery Lazarev.
       p.   cm.
   Includes bibliographical references and index.
   ISBN 0-8179-3942-3 (alk. paper)
   1. Prison industries—Economic aspects—Soviet Union.   2. Forced
labor—Economic aspects—Soviet Union.   3. Soviet Union—Economic
conditions.   4. Industrialization—Soviet Union.   5. Soviet Union—Politics and
government.   I. Gregory, Paul R.   II. Lazarev, V. V. (Valeriǐ Vasil'evich)
HV8931.S65 E26   2003
331.11'73—dc22   2003058318

Cover image courtesy of The Jamestown Foundation and Mr. James V. Kimsey.
The painting is by Gulag artist Nikolai Getman. It depicts the Butara gold-sand
fields where Gulag prisoners were forced to labor year round breaking up the
ground and sifting or panning to separate the gold from the sand. Many died of
exhaustion, malnutrition, and sickness due to the extremely difficult conditions.

Contents

Foreword

Much has been written, and much is still to be written, about the Gulag. We all know of its status as an "archipelago" (in Solzhenitsyn's words) of penal slavery, inflicted on millions and held as a threat over the rest of the population. We know that the Gulag had great human consequences and came to be, as it were, a distillation of the Soviet terror-state. As such it has been an endless source of personal and historical material.

It is a merit of the present book that it concentrates on an aspect of the story that, while not exactly neglected, has been overshadowed—the Gulag's significance in the Soviet economy and in the Communist theoretical approach.

What is recorded here is in fact revealing of the entire Stalinist order. That order envisaged, in the crucial period, a large pool of labor that could be used as the regime wished. This meant that convicts could be sent to, and used in, the most inhospitable areas, to which little free labor could be attracted. And these convicts could easily be redeployed if further prospects proved appealing to the leadership.

Moreover, as the forced labor population increased, this encouraged the leadership in grandiose plans. Even now, most of us do not take enough into account the sheer importance in the Stalinist mind of the subjective drive for spectacular achievements, and along with that drive, the absence of considerations of, and knowledge of, economics.

Thus, besides its penal role, the Gulag was designed from the first to carry out some of the large projects of the planned economy that the USSR was supposed, even sometimes believed, to be putting into practice. This distorted view gives us insight into the connection, or absence of connection, between the minds of the Soviet leaders and reality, above all economic reality. What emerges are not only the economic aspects of the Gulag itself but the huge irrationalities that its existence encouraged.

The Stalinist mindset in the late 1920s and after was not one of thoughtful and careful planning, though it presented itself as such to the world. The Communist leadership, especially Stalin himself, was obsessed with the idea of grand projects that would make the USSR the envy of the world. The Five-Year Plans were issued without serious examination by experts or against their advice (for as long as they survived).

The mania for the grandiose—and the opposition to such schemes from economists, transport experts, even geologists—emerged in the first discussions of the original Five-Year Plan,[1] when forced labor had not yet developed on a vast scale. Among the projects covered were ones such as Magnitogorsk, which was intended to be manned only partly by forced labor and was originally publicized as the greatest of steel works and a model city for prosperous proletarians. The steel works emerged, but the model city failed to follow. Economists pointed out that this "Largest Steel Mill in the World" would be located where fuel had to be delivered from afar, that the deposits might give out (as they did eventually),

---

1. For example, see Loren R. Graham, *The Ghost of the Executed Engineer* (Cambridge: Harvard University Press, 1993).

and so on. This ill-considered crash planning became a feature of the Gulag.

In the end, it has been cogently argued, the USSR, like other backward states, only survived economically because of its oil. (And part of the built-in delusion of technical progress was the imitation or larceny of Western invention and development. The extent of this was remarkable. But the Soviet state never could catch up.)

Thus one of the economic characteristics shown here is the Gulag's effect on, and contribution to, the distortive economic efforts of the regime.

The White Sea–Baltic Canal, of which even Molotov is quoted as being skeptical (dealt with in Chapters 8 and 9), was the first of the enormous Gulag projects. It was completed with great publicity—including a celebration by leading Soviet writers, headed by Maksim Gorky. Prisoners were produced, all of whom spoke of how "corrective" labor had indeed corrected them. This story came out, as noted here, in a book published also in the West. But unfortunately the book had to be withdrawn when one of its heroes, S. G. Firin, the camps' commander, disappeared into the execution cellars with other contributors to the book. (This propaganda operation was never repeated, though deceptions of Westerners and others occasionally occurred). The canal was never of much use— as is true of various later projects. On Stalin's death, a large-scale Arctic railway was abandoned, with camps and even locomotives left on the tundra.

Some of the large Gulag enterprises were profitable, in particular the horrific Kolyma gold mines where the ore was near the surface, though as Nordlander tells us in Chapter 6, later mining had to be done deep down so that the output, compared with the inevitable new expenses, became less impressive.

But generally speaking, there was a flawed calculation at the level of the work, and of the poor fare, of the ordinary prisoner. The misunderstanding of economics that emerges had its source in the idea that forced labor was a powerful and positive resource. Marx had held slave labor to be unprofitable because the slave had no economic incentive. The Gulag was designed to create an incentive—with lower production resulting in lower rations. Though this sounds plausible, it did not work out as planned.

In part Gulag inefficiency was caused by the shortages of real, as against supposed, rations even at the highest work-to-eat level, and in part by the large-scale faking of results—that is to say, the struggle for existence produced at least some element of economic reality.

As demonstrated in these pages, there was always a contradiction between the two objectives of the Gulag—punishment on the one hand, and on the other, exploitation of the victims' labor. In 1937–39, even the residue of rationality in the system disappeared, and the aim of crushing the enemy became paramount: the forced laborer was undergoing retribution and could not even marginally be "coddled" (as Stalin once put it). This led to huge human—and economic—losses, including the wastage of the skilled: a professor of physics is not best used as a shoveler.

Eventually, though inadequately, the general inefficiency of the forced labor system became clear even to its senior operators. As Khlevnyuk notes in Chapter 3, the MVD (Soviet Interior Ministry), especially after Stalin's death, used various economic incentives— in particular, moving part of its workers from forced labor to a form of free labor. But (he notes) these workers were still bound to their jobs and locations and often, in penal exile, were made to report regularly to the police (as had been true under Lenin and Stalin, and with others under the Tsar). This may be regarded (in Khlevnyuk's words) as a transfer from slavery to serfdom—an improvement, but an inadequate one, both economically and otherwise.

In these pages, we see the development of projects large and less large, in which forced labor played a central part. It is not a simple picture, but one that varies in time and place. But viewing these developments together, we find an extraordinary presentation of a major aspect of the Soviet approach to economic achievement—an approach largely vitiated by mental distortions whose results should prove a lesson to the world.

Robert Conquest
Hoover Institution

Acknowledgments

We would like to thank John Raisian, Director of the Hoover Institution on War, Revolution and Peace, for his material and moral support of this publication. The Hoover Institution has a long distinguished record of collecting archival materials, promoting research, and producing publications that deal, in part, with the history of communism in the former Soviet bloc and its eventual demise. We are honored that this volume now joins that heritage. The Lakeside Foundation deserves specific mention for its support of this book project. Additionally, we thank Elena Danielson, Lora Soroka, and Carol Leadenham of the Hoover Archives, as well as Richard Sousa of the Hoover Institution. We, of course, want to express our gratitude to all the contributing authors. For their translation assistance, we thank April Ricks, Steven Shabad, and Natalie Volosovych. And we wish to thank Pat Baker and the staff of the Hoover Press for their excellent and timely work on this publication.

Paul Gregory
Valery Lazarev

Contributors

LEONID BORODKIN is a professor of history at Moscow Lomonosov State University, where he heads the Center for Economic History. He serves as the editor of the *Yearbook of Economic History* and the *Review of Economic History*. Borodkin is a member of the Executive Committee of the International Association for Economic History. He has published extensively on the history of the labor market in both the Russian and Soviet periods.

ROBERT CONQUEST is a senior research fellow at the Hoover Institution, Stanford University. His many awards and honors include the Jefferson Lectureship in the Humanities. He is the author of a number of books on politics, international affairs, and Soviet history, including the classics *The Great Terror* and *The Harvest of Sorrow*, which have appeared in many translations, as has his most recent book, *Reflections on a Ravaged Century*.

SIMON ERTZ is a postgraduate student in modern history, economics, and East European studies at the Free University of Berlin. From 2001 to 2002, he was a visiting fellow at the Center for Economic History at Moscow State University. During that time he conducted intensive research in the Russian archives on the economics of the Gulag.

PAUL GREGORY is the Cullen Distinguished Professor of Economics at the University of Houston, a fellow at the Hoover Institution, and a research professor at the German Institute for Economic Research in Berlin. He has published widely on the Soviet and Russian transition economies, including the monographs *Before Command, Russian National Income, 1885–1913*, and *Soviet and Russian Economic Structure and Performance* (with Robert Stuart), now in its seventh edition. His monograph *The Political Economy of Stalinism* is in press. Gregory is also the editor of *Behind the Façade of Stalin's Command Economy,* published by the Hoover Press.

CHRISTOPHER JOYCE is a research fellow at the Centre for Russian and East European Studies at the University of Birmingham, England. He has recently completed his Ph.D. thesis "The Gulag: 1930–1960" and is working on a regional analysis of the Great Terror. He is also a professional singer and teaches Russian song repertoire at the Birmingham Conservatoire.

OLEG KHLEVNYUK is a senior researcher at the Russian State Archival Service. His principal focus is the history of the Stalin era, and he has published influential books on Stalinism, including *The Politburo: The Mechanism of Political Power in the 1930s* (in Russian) and *In Stalin's Shadow: The Career of Sergo Ordzhonikidze,* in both Russian and English. He has recently finished editing a six-volume collection of Gulag documents.

VALERY LAZAREV is an assistant professor of economics at the University of Houston at Clear Lake, a fellow at the Hoover Institution, and a visiting assistant professor of economics at Yale University. Lazarev has published articles on the Soviet administrative-command system in the *Economic History Review* and in the *Journal of Comparative Economics*. His current research interests include the economic analysis of nondemocratic government and the political economy of postcommunist transition.

MIKHAIL MORUKOV is a postgraduate student at the Institute of Russian History of the Russian Academy of Sciences. He is completing a dissertation on the contribution of the Gulag to the Soviet economy from 1929 to 1945. He has contributed more than ten articles to Russian historical journals on the Gulag system.

DAVID NORDLANDER received his Ph.D. from the University of North Carolina at Chapel Hill and spent two years at Harvard University as a postdoctoral fellow. He works for the Library of Congress's "Meeting of the Frontiers" project on the history of Alaska and Siberia. Nordlander has published his work on the Magadan Gulag in the *Slavic Review*.

ANDREI SOKOLOV is the principal scientific researcher at the Institute of Russian History of the Russian Academy of Sciences and is the director of the Center for Contemporary Russian History. He is the author of a number of monographs, including the two-volume *Course of Soviet History,* and is the coauthor of *Stalinism as a Way of Life*, published in the United States in 2000.

ALEKSEI TIKHONOV serves as business correspondent for the Russian newspaper *Izvestia*. He has been an assistant professor of history at Moscow State University and a visiting fellow at the Hoover Institution, where he studied the Hoover Soviet archives on the topics of defense, the Gulag, and Russian monetary institutions. His work on the monetary reform of the 1930s has been published in the *Journal of Economic History*.

An Introduction to the Economics of the Gulag

Paul Gregory

THE ACRONYM "GULAG" translates as the "Main Administration of Camps," an agency that was subordinate to the USSR Ministry of Interior.[1] The interior ministry operated under four acronyms from the time of the Bolshevik Revolution to Stalin's death in March of 1953. It was first known as the Cheka, under its first minister, Feliks Dzherzhinsky. It was renamed the OGPU in 1922. The OGPU was merged into the NKVD in 1934. The NKVD was headed by G. G. Yagoda (from 1934 to 1936), N. I. Yezhov (from 1936 to 1938), and L. P. Beria (from 1938 to 1945). It was renamed the MVD in 1946. Although the interior ministry had three other ministers before Stalin's death, the bloody history of the Cheka-OGPU-NKVD-MVD is associated with these four leaders, of whom only Dzerzhinsky escaped execution and died of natural causes. The Great Purges of 1937–38 are usually referred

1. The author is particularly grateful to Aleksei Tikhonov who collected much of the statistical material cited in this chapter from the Soviet Gulag archives of the Hoover Institution.

to as the "Yezhovschina" after the zealous NKVD minister who spearheaded them.[2]

The generic term "Gulag" refers to the vast system of prisons, camps, psychiatric hospitals, and special laboratories that housed the millions of prisoners, or *zeks*. Although Soviet propaganda at times praised the Gulag's rehabilitation of anti-Soviet elements through honest labor, there were no Soviet studies of the Gulag. The interior ministry had to turn to studies written in the West, which have been carefully preserved in its archives.[3] Broad public understanding of the magnitude and brutality of the Gulag was generated by the publication of Alexander Solzhenitsyn's *The Gulag Archipelago*.[4] Since Russian independence many historical and political works have been published in Russia along with the memoirs of former prisoners. Former camp administrators have remained silent, so we have no accounts from the perspective of the camps' bosses.

THE GULAG AS AN INSTITUTION OF THE TOTALITARIAN STATE

This book is a collection of studies of forced labor in the Soviet Union until the time of Stalin's death and its immediate aftermath. These studies focus mainly on the most extreme form of coercion— penal labor, but they also describe the application of force in the everyday workplace, a practice prominent from the late 1930s through the end of World War II. The extensive political and social literature that exists today on the Gulag has chronicled the suffering and loss of life it caused, establishing beyond a doubt the Gulag's

2. Marc Jansen and Nikita Petrov, *Stalin's Loyal Executioner, People's Commissar Nikolai Ezhov, 1895–1940* (Stanford: Hoover Press, 2001).

3. Oleg Khlevnyuk, "The Economy of the Gulag" in *Behind the Façade of Stalin's Command Economy,* ed. Paul Gregory (Stanford: Hoover Press, 2001), 111.

4. Alexander Solzhenitsyn, *The Gulag Archipelago*, 3 vols. (New York: Harper and Row, 1973).

brutality and criminality. Our focus is on the Gulag as an institution of coercive power in a totalitarian state. We are interested in its functions and operations, both formal and informal, and its contributions to the goals of the dictator. We are interested in whether the Gulag was created to serve the economic interests of the totalitarian state or whether it was a by-product of the dictator's consolidation of power.

The Soviet administrative-command system was the most important experiment of the twentieth century. Its true operation, hidden behind a vast veil of secrecy, was exposed by the opening of formerly secret archives. Studies using these archives reveal that the system's working arrangements were more complex and subtle than had been imagined.[5] We must examine the institution of the Soviet Gulag in a similar light to determine its true working arrangements.

The chapters in this book are based mainly on research in the archives of the Gulag, in its central, regional, and local archives. Three chapters examine the general institutions of force and coercion as applied to labor (Chapters 2, 3, and 4). Four chapters are devoted to case studies of three major Gulag projects (The White Sea–Baltic Canal in Chapter 8, Magadan in Chapter 6, the Karelia region in Chapter 9, and the Norilsk Metallurgy Complex in Chapter 7). Chapter 5 examines the use of penal labor in Norilsk. The case studies use both central and local archives, while the studies of central institutions use the central archives of the Gulag and the relevant central archives of the Soviet state and party.[6] These archives are located in Moscow and in the regions themselves. The

5. See, for example, Paul Gregory, *The Political Economy of Stalinism: New Evidence from the Secret Soviet Archives* (New York: Cambridge University Press, 2003).

6. S. A. Krasilnikov, "Rozhdenie Gulaga: diskussia v verkhnikh eschelonakh vlasti: Postanovlenia Politburo TsK VKP(b), 1929–1930," *Istoricheskiy Arkhiv.* 1997, N 4, pp. 142–56.

Gulag archives are also located in the collections of the Hoover Institution.

The archive documents tell the complicated story of how the forced labor system was created and operated partly by design and partly by learning from experience. Internal reports on the state of the Gulag reveal a high level of introspection by top Gulag administrators and give a valuable insider's view of the Gulag's strengths and weaknesses.

Internal Gulag documents reveal three constants of Gulag administration. First, the Gulag's structure and development were dictated by the political strategy of the dictatorship. As noted by a Gulag administrator: "Organizational changes within the Gulag are normally caused by external political and/or economic decisions of the state."[7] The Gulag was populated as a consequence of the exogenous state policies of collectivization, the Great Terror, the harsh labor laws, and the imprisonment of returning POWs. From 1934 on, the Gulag had to manage the "unplanned" rise in the number of prisoners and the simultaneous expansion of the prison camp network. The Gulag's attempts at advance planning grossly underestimated the influx of prisoners. Its planners consistently expected a diminishing number of prisoners. The third Five-Year Plan (1938–42), which was drawn up during the Great Purges, remarkably projected fewer prisoners just as the first victims of the Great Terror began flooding in.

The second constant was the economic raison d'être of the Gulag: the exploration and industrial colonization of remote resource-rich regions at a low cost of society's resources. As noted by an internal Gulag document: "The history of the Gulag is the history of the colonization and industrial exploitation of the remote regions of the state."[8] Although prison labor was used throughout

7. 9414-1-368, l.115. (Hoover Archives)
8. 9414-1-368, l.115.

the USSR, Gulag labor was principally concentrated in remote regions that had difficult climates and that would have been costly to settle with free labor. The use of penal labor in remote regions was supposed to achieve economic "surpluses" (similar to Marx's surplus value) by paying unfree labor only subsistence wages (or paying well below the rate for free labor) to produce products that had substantial economic value. Penal labor was supposed to be more mobile than hired labor because prisoners could be shifted in large numbers from one project to another. Penal labor was also supposed to provide surpluses and resource mobility without the loss of labor productivity. Close supervision and monitoring, it was hoped, would render penal labor as productive as free labor.

The third constant was the conflict between the economic function of the Gulag and its function of isolating prisoners from the general population and preventing escapes. The more prisoners were used for construction and production, which required their movement from job to job or from task to task, the weaker the security regime. Prisoners contracted out to civilian enterprises and institutions were particularly difficult to guard, to isolate from the general population, and to prevent from escaping. To a degree, the Gulag attempted to reduce the friction between its isolation and economic functions by locating production facilities close to the place of confinement, but this was an expensive solution. All the economic tasks that inmates were supposed to carry out could not be located within the confines of camps. As the Gulag's economic system became more complicated and its economic obligations heavier, "its priority function of protection and isolation was negatively affected," as remarked one Gulag chronicler.[9]

The chapters in this book show the struggle within the dictatorship and within the Gulag between the notion that productive

9. "Vozniknovenie i Razvitie ITL, ULAGa i GULAGa OGPU-NKVD-MKVD SSSR" - 9414-1-369 (3.4708) l.129.

labor can be extracted by coercion and the realization that people must be offered "carrots" as well as "sticks" if they are to work well. Chapter 2 shows that the Soviet leadership sought in vain the right balance between carrots and sticks in the "civilian" labor force and often combined extreme coercion with extreme material incentives. Chapters 3, 5, 6, and 9 show that material incentives played an ever larger role in motivating penal labor, and Chapter 4 shows that in the last few years of the Gulag, distinctions between free and penal labor were blurred. Chapter 5 shows that eventually prisoners had to be offered material incentives that were distributed among prisoners much as they were distributed among civilian workers. Although prison bosses had an arsenal of tools to motivate prisoners to fulfill their plans—punishment, sentence reductions for good work, moral incentives, and material incentives—they learned that coercion alone was not sufficient. There were, moreover, complicated tradeoffs: prisoners placed on reduced rations for failing to meet their quotas were no longer able to work effectively because of their weakened state. One of the most effective incentive systems—reduced sentences as a reward for exemplary work—deprived the Gulag of its best workers through their early release.

THE ORGANIZATIONAL STRUCTURE OF THE GULAG

In the chapters that follow, there are references to many organizations related to the Gulag—the OGPU, NKVD, MVD, Gulag main administrations, economic administrations, and regional organizations. We have already explained that the OGPU, MKVD, and MVD were, in effect, different names for the Soviet interior ministry, or the state security ministry, which was the superior of the Gulag administration. To simplify the discussion that follows, we shall use the best-known designation of the interior ministry of the Stalin era—the NKVD. As Figure 1.1 shows, the NKVD received its orders from the highest political and party authority, the Council of Peo-

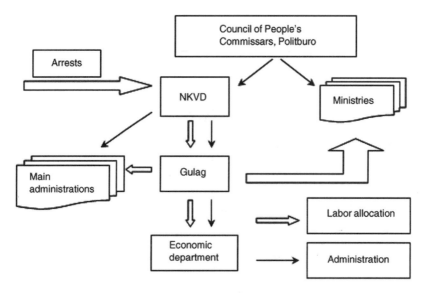

Figure 1.1   Organizational Structure of the Gulag

ple's Commissars (the highest state body) and the Politburo (the highest body of the Communist Party). Like industrial ministries, the NKVD was broken down into main administrations, called *glavki*, which were responsible for carrying out the functions of state security. This book is about the NKVD's most notorious main administration, the Main Administration of Camps, or Gulag.

Figure 1.1 illustrates the structure and relationships of the Gulag. The Gulag received its orders from the NKVD, that is, from the minister of interior, such as Yezhov or Beria. The head of Gulag administration was responsible for carrying out these orders and directives. The supply of prisoners was delivered by the courts and justice ministries to the NKVD, and delivered by the NKVD to the Gulag. The Gulag served as a "labor intermediary" by distributing penal labor to its own main industrial administrations, or Gulag *glavki,* or to the economic administrations that it administered directly. The Gulag could also contract penal labor out to other construction and industrial production ministries. Because it had

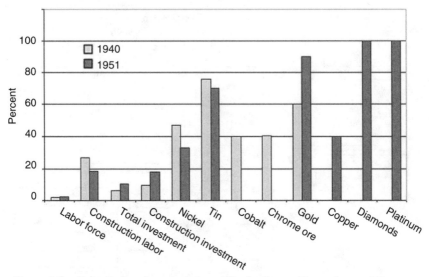

Figure 1.2   Gulag Labor, Investment, and Production as Percentages of the Total Economy (1940 and 1951)
Sources: Gulag labor is from Table 1.2. The total labor including construction labor is from Warren Eason, "Labor Force," *Economic Trends in the Soviet Union*, ed. Abram Bergson and Simon Kuznets (Cambridge: Harvard University Press, 1963), 77, 82. Gulag construction labor is calculated at 75 percent of the total, following Table 5. Gulag investment figures are from GARF 9414-1-28, 9414-1-1312, 9414-1-188. The overall investment figures are from Richard Moorsteen and Raymond Powell, *The Soviet Capital Stock, 1928–1962* (Homewood, Ill.: Richard D. Irwin, 1966), 391. The mineral production shares are from G. M. Ivanova, *Gulag v sisteme totalitarnogo gosudarstva* (Moscow, 1997), 97.

its own construction and production responsibilities and because Gulag *glavki*, although quasi-independent, had to meet their plan goals, the Gulag had to weigh the financial benefit of contracting labor to third parties against the need for prisoners in its own production structure.

Almost all prisoners were confined either in Corrective Labor Camps, called ITLs, or in labor colonies, also known as general places of confinement. Henceforth we refer to the first as "camps" and the second as "colonies." Some prisoners were confined to mental institutions, high-security prisons, special research facilities (for elite scientists and engineers) or special camps. Camps provided traditional prisonlike confinement with guards and strict supervision of prisoners. Colonies were located in remote regions, and "colonists" were prevented from leaving by lack of transport and by internal passport rules. The term of custody was the decisive formal criterion for the kind of confinement: "In accordance with criminal laws (Article 28 of the Criminal Codex of the Russian Republic), the Corrective labor camps (ITL) are for those prisoners sentenced to terms of three years or more."[10]

Before the control of forced labor was unified under the NKVD in 1934, camps and colonies were administered both by the USSR interior ministry and by republican organizations (republican justice ministries and republican NKVDs). The first and most famous prison camp, the Solovetsky Camp of Special Destination (SLON), was founded in 1920 on Dzherzhinsky's (the first head of the Cheka) initiative[11] to isolate counterrevolutionaries. The systematic use of forced labor began in 1926 and was at first limited to forestry and fisheries in the local environs.[12] Starting with the first Five-Year Plan (1928–33), the OGPU was the agency of colonization. On July 11, 1929, the Council of People's Commissars created the Administrative Authority of Northern Camps of Special Destination (USLON) of the OGPU for the exploitation of mineral resources in the northern territories. Such remote camps colonized undeveloped regions and isolated individuals posing threats to the socialist state. The emerging network of the prison camp administration was created independently of the existing territorial prison administration system operated by the justice ministry and territorial authorities. As a result, the administration of prison camps was in fact divided into two parts: the OGPU, which distributed the prisoners among the

10. 9414-1-502, l.158.
11. 9414-1-368, l.118.
12. 9414-1-368, l.118.

Table 1.1   Gulag Camps Created in 1932

Project	Location	Task
Belomor-Baltisky (White Sea–Baltic)	Karelia	Construction of the White Sea channel
Severo-Vostochny (Northeast)	Kolyma River	Development of the Far East and production of nonferrous metals
Prorvinsky	Kazakhstan	Fishery
Dmitrovsky	Moscow region	Construction of the Moscow-Volga channel
Baikal-Amursky	Far East	Railroad construction

camps, and the territorial administrative organs, which were responsible for their utilization. Newly created camps, such as the notable camp complexes founded in 1932 (listed in Table 1.1), were subordinate to the OGPU.[13]

The Gulag system was concentrated under the NKVD, in 1934, under its Gulag administration.[14] Under this unified administration, inmate numbers soared, as did Gulag responsibilities. Many projects begun by civil administrations were shifted to the Gulag, eventually overwhelming its administrative capacities, as a 1940 report indicated: "The Gulag has 30 main building projects; none will be completed in 1940. All will continue for several years, with an overall labor budget of 14.7 million rubles. The Gulag is systematically charged with additional building projects, which result in a remarkable backlog. The large number of construction projects requires a fundamental reorganization, and the magnitude of these tasks complicates management in an extreme fashion, leading to a diversification of tasks and to bottlenecks in resource allocation."[15]

To administer its increasingly complicated production and construction complexes, the Gulag created in 1941 the main economic

13. 9414-1-368, l.120.
14. *Sobranie Zakonov SSSR-1934*, No. 56, p.421 (see 9414-1-368, ll.117-118).
15. 9414-1-2990, l.5.

administrations, also called *glavki,* to take responsibility for its economic activities.[16] These newly founded administrations guided economic branches, except Dalstroi (Far Northern Construction), which administered 130 separate camp facilities in a territory covering 3 million square kilometers (see Chapter 6). The Gulag's complex structure gave observers the impression of several Gulags developing in the prewar USSR.

World War II reduced the number of prisoners because of transfers to the front and increased mortality, and the number of Gulag organizations declined (see Chapters 2 and 3). Although the Gulag administration expected a continued decline at the end of the war, there was a new influx of returning POWs, wartime collaborators, and inmates sentenced under new criminal codes. Both the number of inmates and the Gulag's economic activities expanded again after 1947.[17] Inmate totals reached their peak at 2.5 million in the early 1950s. Table 1.2 presents a general picture of the Gulag on the eve of World War II, at the end of the war, and in the early 1950s. The increase in the Gulag bureaucracy appeared to outrun the increase in the number of prisoners. The ratio of guards to inmates rose after the war to almost one guard for every ten inmates. These ratios

16. The main economic administrations (*glavki*) independent from the Gulag were founded by decree No. 00212 February 26, 1941, by the NKVD. They consisted of the following:
    GUShDS (Main Administration of Railroad Construction)
    GUGidroStroi (Main Administration of Hydraulic Construction / Engineering)
    GULGMP (Main Administration of Camps in Mining and Metallurgical Industry)
    GULPS (Main Administration of Camps for Industrial Construction)
    ULTP (Administration of Camps in Heavy Industry)
    ULLP (Administration of Camps in Forestry and Wood Processing)
    Administration of Construction of the Kuibishew Industry Plants
    Dalstroi (Far Eastern Construction Trust)
    GULSchosDor (Main Administration of Camps for Highway Construction)
17. See Chapter 5 (this volume).

Table 1.2   Numbers of Prisoners and Camps (First of Year)

	1941	1947	1951	1953
Total number of inmates (millions)	1.9	1.7	2.5	2.5
Prisoners in camps (millions)	1.5	0.8	1.5	1.7
Total number of camps	76	56	115	158
Number of main administrations	9	6	12	15
Guards (thousands)	107	91	223	257
Ratio of guards to inmates	5.6	5.3	8.9	10.2

Sources: 1941: 9414-1-368, 9414-1-1155, 9414-1-28 (Hoover archives); 1947: 9414-1-86; 1951: 9414-1-112; 1953: 9414-1-507.

must be interpreted with caution because a high proportion of guards were themselves inmates (see Chapter 5).

THE GULAG AS THE SUPPLIER OF PENAL LABOR

Throughout the many changes in administration, responsibilities, and inmate totals, the Gulag remained the sole centralized administrator of the camp sector or guard regime. As such, it was the monopoly supplier of prison labor to the economy. As noted by one of the Gulag's chief administrators: "The Gulag ensures the required labor force replenishment of the building projects and industrial plants of the MVD by supplying prisoners to the appropriate camps and colonies. At the same time, the Gulag provides manpower for civilian ministries on a contractual basis in order to organize special colonies for prisoners next to the industrial location and building projects of these ministries."[18] All colonies and several agricultural camps remained under the direct control of the Gulag itself, including special camps for counterrevolutionaries, which were founded in 1948 and which required a special disciplinary regime.

Table 1.3 shows the distribution of prison labor by the *glavki*,

18. 9414-1-374, l.55.

Table 1.3   Distribution of Prison Labor (1941, 1947, 1950, 1953)

Main Glavki	Function	Number of Inmates (Thousands)			
		1941	1947	1950	1953
GULZhDS	Railroad construction	486	192	294	205
Glavpromstroi	Military construction	204	124	183	382
Glavgidrostroi	Hydraulic construction/ engineering	193	0	46	119
GULGMP	Metal mining	158	173	224	242
Dalstroi	Far North construction	184	102	153	175
GULLP	Forestry	318	244	280	322
GUShosDor	Highways	25	0	24	20
Third Department	Gulag production (special camps and colonies)	704	1,168	1,320	986
Contract workers	Hired out	255	469	636	273
Total MVD		2,290	2,027	2,561	2,482

Note that the numbers involve some double counting; perhaps forestry workers are included both in the forestry *glavki* and in Third Department workers.
Sources: Various documents from 9414 -1 and (Systema ITL . . ., M.1996).

by the Gulag's own operations (the Third Department), and by the prisoners contracted out to civilian enterprises. For the early 1950s, of the 2.5 million prisoners, between 1 and 1.3 million worked in the Gulag's Third Department, between a quarter and a half million were hired out, and the rest worked mainly in forestry, railroad construction, military production, hydroelectric power, and Far North construction. The Third Department was the largest economic subdivision of the Gulag, accounting for more than one-third of all prison labor for more than a decade. Besides gold mining, the Third Department included several old Gulag camps, most of the Special Camps founded in 1948, and all general places of confinement, including colonies whose administration was carried out by the territorial departments and subdivisions of the Gulag. The untold story of Table 1.3 is the five hundred thousand to six hundred thousand penal workers contracted out to civilian employers in the early postwar years. Although they constituted a relatively small share of the Soviet labor force, they were concentrated largely in construction and thus constituted a much higher share of total construction employment.

Although the criminal codex required that prisoners sentenced to fewer than three years be imprisoned in colonies, the Gulag openly defied this law when it faced labor bottlenecks. From the Gulag's perspective, those sentenced to colonies were less valuable because the transport of prisoners to remote colonies could take up to half a year. Hence, the most significant projects were not carried out in colonies. Special decrees allowed the MVD "to displace prisoners sentenced to a term of custody of up to two years from colonies to camps."[19] A memorandum written for the Gulag administration in July of 1947 found that 13 percent of the inmates in camps had been sentenced to terms of custody of fewer than three years, while more than half of all prisoners in colonies were sentenced to more than three years and should have been in camps.

As the Gulag and civilian employers wrestled for penal workers, the MVD and its Gulag administration resisted calls for more civilian control of penal workers. State policy sometimes favored the Gulag, sometimes the industrial ministries. A government decree of November 4, 1947, forbade the assignment of prisoners to civilian projects without MVD-Gulag approval, stipulating that prisoners be sent on a priority basis to the Far North and Far East, where it was difficult to procure free labor. Another state decree obliged the MVD-Gulag to provide labor from special contingents without

---

19. 9414-1-1170, l.1.

prior agreement with the MVD.[20] Open battles broke out between the Gulag and the civilian ministries. In 1950, the economic ministries claimed the Gulag "owed" them 125,000 prisoners, while the Gulag accused the ministries of withholding 33,000 prisoners.[21] The ministries lobbied for prime prison labor, while the Gulag supplied a representative cross-section of prisoners with regard to sex, age, qualification, and health. The Gulag preferred to supply women, elderly workers, and unskilled workers, imposing social obligations linked to these categories of prisoners on the hiring enterprise. Frequent quarrels over nonpayments required Council of Ministers intervention, such as the April 21, 1947, special order that ministries pay outstanding debts to the MVD, which could demand its prisoners back if payments were overdue more than one month. As the decree ordered: "These accounts have to be paid from the funds reserved for the payment of the regular wages for workers and employees." Nonpaying enterprises had to pay transport costs back to the prisoners' places of confinement.[22]

The Gulag's supply of labor to civilian employers depended on the influx of prisoners. When the number of prisoners entering the Gulag dropped sharply in 1951, the number of inmates contracted out to outside employers also fell sharply. As stated by a Gulag report: "As a result of the decrease in inflow of newly sentenced contingents, the number of prisoners assigned to other ministries also sharply declined. Within one year alone from November 1, 1950 to November 1, 1951, their number declined by more than a third."[23] When caught with a labor shortage, the Gulag endeavored to cut supplies to other ministries. A new inflow of prisoners after 1951 led to a new rise in building activity. Stakes were high in

20. 9414-1-112, l.39.
21. 9414-1-112, l.26.
22. 9414-1-1271, (f. 3.5086), l.66 (Circulation letter from the Chief of the Gulag to local administrators of camps and colonies, May 4, 1947).
23. 9414-1-3712, l.169.

disputes between the Gulag and civilian employers because of the large numbers of prisoners involved. Table 1.4 shows that prison labor could account for up to 18 percent of total employment in some civilian sectors, such as heavy industry construction.

Table 1.5 divides the 1950 Gulag labor-staffing plan into construction, industry, and contract employment. It shows that 27 percent of Gulag labor was classified as "free," although there is considerable doubt as to how "free" such labor was (see Chapter 5). More "free" laborers worked in industry than in the harsh conditions of construction. Most contracted-out inmate labor went to construction. Hence, if we add all contracted workers to construction, we find that penal labor accounted for 81 percent of workers in Gulag construction projects, while only 19 percent of free labor worked in construction projects. In Gulag documents, these free workers are explicitly mentioned as *labor force,* so this figure does not include either administrative employees or guards. Thus the Gulag hired free labor in production while contracting out prisoners to the external construction sector. The number of free laborers working in Gulag industry approximately equaled the number of prisoners "exported" for outside construction employment

The Gulag's use of "free" labor contradicts both the stereotype of the Gulag and the minister of the interior's report to Stalin, G. Malenkov, and Beria, which stated that "all orders concerning large-scale construction and industrial production given to the Gulag are executed by prisoners."[24] The Gulag may have exaggerated the role of prisoners in this instance to claim more budget resources. The Gulag also expected budget subsidies for nonworking and disabled prisoners. One document complained: "In fact, the donation from the budget was lower than the expenses for the maintenance of the non-working prisoners and just covered the

24. 9414-1-118, l.4.

Table 1.4 Contract Assignments of Prison Labor Force

November 1946			July 1950		
Ministry	Number	%	Ministry	Number	%
Building projects in heavy industry	45,940	11.9	Heavy construction	104,943	18.0
Fuel industry	39,772	10.3	Coal industry	76,893	13.2
Nonferrous metallurgy	29,886	7.7	Power plants	51,511	8.8
Coal industry (west and east)	21,641	5.6	Small engineering	41,628	7.1
Transport	20,921	5.4	Oil industry	31,392	5.4
Military and naval industry	19,772	5.1	Wood processing and paper industry	30,597	5.2
Aviation industry	18,213	4.7	Metallurgical industry	25,855	4.4
Power plants	14,841	3.8	Aviation industry	15,249	2.6
Automotive engineering	12,683	3.3	Chemical industry	13,898	2.4
Ferrous metallurgy	12,505	3.2	Food industry	13,563	2.3
Food industry	11,908	3.1	Transportation	13,555	2.3
Special food products	11,420	2.9	Agricultural engineering	13,354	2.3
Wood processing agricultural	11,335	2.9	Building materials industry	12,140	2.1
Engineering	11,204	2.9	Automotive engineering	10,532	1.8
Building materials industry	10,033	2.6	House-building industry	9,726	1.7
Textile industry	7,879	2.0	Civil construction	9,413	1.6
Civil construction	6,644	1.7	Car and tractor industry	9,172	1.6
Other	80,934	19.2	Other	99,780	16.1
Civilian sector	387,531	91.7	Civilian sector	583,201	94.2
Contracted to MVD	35,045	8.3	Contracted to MVD	39,903	6.4
Total	422,576	100	Total	619,274	100

Sources: 1946: 9414-1-2114, I.33, 1950: 9414-1-1343, II.96-98.

Table 1.5   Employment in Construction and Industry of Gulag Labor according to 1950 Plan (Thousands of People)

Category of Labor	(1) Industry		(2) Construction		(3) Hired to Outside Employers		(4) Implied Construction (2+3)		(5) Total Employment, Gulag Labor	
	Number	Percent	Number	Percent	Number	Percent	Number	Percent	Number	Percent
Penal	739	63	596	69	584	100	1180	81	1919	73
Free	437	37	270	31			270	19	707	27
Total labor	1176	100	866	100	584	100	1450	100	2626	100
Percentage distribution by employment activity	45		33		22		55		100	

Source: 9414-1-1312. The calculations presented above are based on the data of the "projected plan of the average annual labor requirements of the industrial and construction sectors for 1950," drawn up by the planning department of the MVD.

expenses for the maintenance of disabled persons and prisoners kept in transit camps until their forwarding to the camps and colonies."[25] Beginning in 1948, there were repeated attempts by the MVD to incorporate the Gulag directly into the state budget to obtain automatic subsidies.[26]

THE GEOGRAPHY OF THE GULAG

The Gulag's camps, colonies, prisons, labs, and mental hospitals were dispersed across the vast expanse of the USSR. Although Gulag operations, such as the construction of the metro deep underneath Moscow, took place in major metropolitan centers, the large Gulag camps and colonies (listed in Chapter 3), which employed tens of

25. 9414-1-118, l.4.
26. 9414-1-334 Report by the minister of interior S. Kryglov including a similar proposal written in 1948.

thousands of prisoners, shared one feature: they were located in the northern and eastern parts of the Soviet Union in harsh climates, far from civilization and transport. Geographical remoteness allowed prisoners to be isolated from the rest of the population and reduced the cost of security. However, the main reason for location in the Far North and Far East was the presence of such valuable resources as Norilsk's nickel ores (see Chapter 7), Magadan's gold ores (see Chapter 6), or the forestry reserves of Siberia, which all required large infrastructure investments to develop and which were shunned by free labor.

Figure 1.3 provides a map of the major Gulag camps and colonies covered in this book. It clearly shows the skewed geographical distribution of camps and colonies to the north and east.

THE GULAG'S ECONOMIC CONTRIBUTION

The Gulag held somewhat fewer than 2 million prisoners in its colonies and camps in 1940. This number peaked at 2.5 million in the early 1950s after former POWs and other returnees from the war were added to the list of Gulag inmates. Thus, in an economy that employed nearly 100 million people, the Gulag accounted for two out of every hundred workers (see Figure 1.2). This percentage could overstate the Gulag's share of labor because it includes invalids and other nonworking inmates. However, we have already shown that the Gulag had a larger number of "free" workers; so the 2 percent figure is a reasonable estimate. The Gulag was charged with some of the most difficult tasks of the economy, such as heavy construction and work in harsh climates and remote regions, which would have required exceptional pay and effort to attract free labor. Some two-thirds of Gulag economic activity was in construction, often in remote and cold regions where transport was difficult. Although Gulag labor accounted for some 2 percent of the labor force, it accounted for about one in five construction workers in

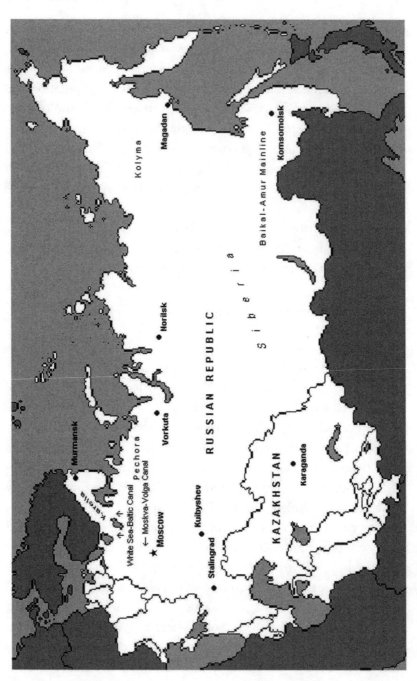

Figure 1.3   Major Gulag Camps and Colonies

1940 and 1951. While accounting for between 6 to 10 percent of total investment, its share of construction investment was almost 20 percent in 1951. In fact, these figures understate the Gulag's role in construction because, in 1938, 30 percent of the Gulag's construction budget was hidden in civilian construction ministries.[27] Gulag production of the most precious minerals, such as gold and diamonds, reached close to 100 percent (as Figure 1.2 shows).

The Gulag system was a by-product of collectivization, the Great Purges, draconian labor policies, and the aftermath of World War II. It would be contrary to script if Stalin and his political allies had not regarded the resulting pool of inmates as a remarkable economic opportunity. Stalin presumed that surpluses could be extracted from Gulag labor similar to those extracted from the peasants of the early 1930s, who were supposed to deliver grain without compensation. In effect, the presumption was that penal workers could be forced to work efficiently and conscientiously without being offered real material incentives. Chapters 2 and 5 show the degree to which these expectations were not realized. These chapters show that penal workers had to be offered wages and monetary bonuses, thus raising their cost to the state.

27. GARF 9414-1-1139.

Forced Labor in Soviet Industry: The End of the 1930s to the Mid-1950s

An Overview

Andrei Sokolov

SOVIET INDUSTRIAL LABOR policies combined coercion with material and moral, or intangible, incentives.[1] Although the mix changed over time, one form of labor motivation never completely dominated. The industrialization drive of the first Five-Year Plan (1928–32) did generate enthusiasm among workers, but expectations remained unfulfilled, and the removal of "class enemies," threatening Stalin's promised "happy" and "merry" life, yielded no improvements. The Stakhanovite campaign to encourage individual feats of labor heroism in 1935 and 1936 failed to raise labor productivity. It was not until after the Great Terror of 1937 and 1938 that the balance shifted toward force and coercion in the workplace. Yet even during the most coercive periods, material and moral incentives were used and even intensified.

Concern about labor discipline is common in countries undergoing rapid industrialization, but the problem was more complicated in the Soviet Union. First, the mass flight of the rural population to the cities because of forced collectivization created

1. Concerning labor stimulation in the 1930s, see A. K. Sokolov, "Sovetskaia Politika v Oblasti Motivatsii i Stimulirovania Truda (1917–1930s)," *Ekonomicheskaia Istoria*, 2000, No. 4.

an industrial labor force with no factory experience and with its own ideas of discipline. The priority of heavy industry required heavy manual labor by both skilled and unskilled labor, but the emphasis on heavy industry meant that there were few consumer goods to motivate labor. The high turnover rate of industrial workers *(tekuchest')* remained a persistent sore point. As long as workers were free to change jobs in "free" local labor markets, planners could not direct and hold workers to complete planned tasks. Administrative recruitment could not direct sufficient labor according to staffing plans, and actual labor distributions diverged from planned tasks. Workers tied to factories for a period after completing their education failed to observe their obligations and sought out other employment.

MORE "STICKS" THAN "CARROTS"

The causes of the economic slowdown of the late 1930s, called "the economic fever," following the successful second Five-Year Plan (1933–37), remain obscure. The growth of military industry "to strengthen the military preparedness of the world's first state of workers and peasants" was one factor. Automatic deductions were taken from workers' pay for the "motorization of the red army," and the budget shifted from investment to defense. Regardless of the slowdown's actual causes, the Soviet leadership decided the slowdown was caused mainly by "worker relationships" and was determined to apply force and coercion to improve discipline in the workplace. Among Soviet leaders the opinion was widely held that "the 'ruling class' [workers] had become impudent" and that it was "time to tighten the screws." The decision to apply force in the workplace was accompanied by the vast growth of penal labor as the Gulag filled with the victims of the Great Purges. The construction of large projects and the opening of new regions with prison labor reinforced the notion that economic problems could be decided by force.

Laws passed in the late 1930s and early 1940s provided the legal basis for draconian measures against industrial workers. On December 20, 1938, the Council of People's Commissars (the highest state body) approved the decree "On the obligatory introduction of work books in all enterprises and institutions," a law designed to attack labor turnover and to reduce the free movement of labor among enterprises. Labor contracts were increased to five-year terms; all job changes, salary and reward histories, punishments, rebukes, and reasons for firings were registered in the labor book, which the cadres department used to evaluate workers' performance. In January of 1939, the Council of People's Commissars decreed that tardiness of 20 minutes or more constituted an unauthorized absence from work. On June 26, 1940, the Presidium of the Supreme Soviet approved the decree "On the transition to an eight hour work day, a seven day work week, and the prohibition of voluntary departures of workers from enterprises and institutions." The June 1940 law tied the worker to the enterprise and introduced criminal punishments for laziness, poor discipline, and tardiness. In August of 1940, criminal punishments were introduced for minor workplace infractions, such as drunkenness, hooliganism, and petty theft. The October 1940 reforms of vocational education raised the term of obligatory work after graduation to four years and prohibited voluntary departures. In some schools, criminal punishments were given for discipline violations and for unauthorized leaves.

Although later conveniently interpreted as necessary preparations for war, these harsh labor measures were passed more than one year before the surprise Nazi invasion of June 22, 1941. Soviet propaganda depicted the increased force in the workplace as an initiative from the workers themselves. On the eve of the passage of the 1940 labor decrees, the plenum of trade unions gave official support for battles against laziness, drunkards, and thieves. Meetings organized in factories and enterprises supposedly enthusiastically supported the new labor laws. Western authors and some contemporary Russian historians, in contrast, regard the move to force and coercion as a natural consequence of the logic of a totalitarian state but ignore the fact that economic methods of labor motivation remained in use. In reality, the Soviet leadership was engaged in the difficult balancing act of attempting to raise labor productivity by combining different methods of labor motivation, swinging between force and economic motivation.

At the same time as force and coercion were increasing, economic incentives were being raised. In the three years leading up to war, worker pay rose substantially. In 1937 a minimum wage of 110 to 115 rubles a month was established. In 1940 alone, the wage fund rose more than 50 percent; the wages of manual ferrous metallurgical workers rose 11 percent; and the wages of engineering-technical workers, 28 percent. The average monthly pay of workers was 331 rubles a month, with engineering-technical workers earning 696 rubles.[2] As a further indicator of the importance of economic incentives, pay scales were further differentiated to reward skilled workers in priority industries. Skilled technical workers were paid twice as much as unskilled workers. Since workers spent 55 percent of their income on food,[3] the Council of People's Commissars on October 7, 1940, allowed workers to farm small garden plots, and in a short time, one million workers were farming private plots, which held one-third of the nation's cows and pigs.[4] In 1937, a commission for the safety of workers was created that introduced factory inspectors; large factories opened their own clinics. By 1938,

2. A. V. Mitrofanova, *Rabochii Klass SSSR Nakanune i v Gody Velikoy Otechestvenno Voiny, 1938–1945 gg* (Moscow: Nauka, 1984), 128.
3. Ibid., 129.
4. Ibid., 132.

1,838 sanatoriums and 1,270 "houses of rest" were in use. On the eve of the war, enterprises supported twelve thousand camps for young pioneers.[5] Only party personnel, highly trained specialists, leading scientific workers, and "leading workers" were assigned individual apartments. Most workers lived in crowded communal apartments and dormitories. In 1940, the average worker in a large Moscow automotive plant was assigned 4.5 square meters of living space.[6] The opportunity for a leading worker to receive an apartment was therefore a formidable incentive. On December 27, 1939, the "Hero of Socialist Labor" award was established, which provided opportunities to enter the party or receive promotions. Such rewards could be individual or collective. For example, the factory "Hammer and Sickle" received the Lenin Medal for its service to the building of socialism in 1939.

Measures passed on the eve of World War II used both "carrots" (wage differentials, the promise of better housing, medals that opened up new career paths) and "sticks" (criminal punishments for minor labor infractions). These measures do not appear to be part of the logical plan of a calculating totalitarian state but its ad hoc responses to problems that were often caused by the state's own actions. New laws were carried out in the form of "campaigns," creating permanent and extraordinary agencies, commissions, and committees, which acquired their own logic and carried measures to absurd extremes. This "campaignism" can be seen in the directives passed to strengthen discipline and order (see Table 2.1).[7]

The sentencing of workers for unauthorized absences and idleness reached its peak well before the German attack. In 1940 alone, of the 3.3 million cases before the People's Courts, 2.1 million were

5. Ibid.
6. Ibid., 133.
7. Compiled from the database published in V. N. Zemskov, "Ukaz ot 26 Iunia 1940 g . . . . (Esche Odna Kruglaia Data)," *Raduga*, 1990, No. 6, p. 46.

Table 2.1   Number Convicted by Court Institutions and Military Tribunals for Lateness, Absenteeism, and Unauthorized Leaving a Workplace, 1940–52

Years	Convicted by courts for absenteeism and lateness of more than 20 min. (according to the law of 26 July 1940)	Convicted by courts for unauthorized leaving a workplace (according to the law of 26 July 1940)	Convicted by military tribunals and courts for unauthorized leaving a workplace (according to martial law of December 1941)
1940	1,769,790	311,648	—
1941	1,458,115	310,967	—
1942	1,274,644	297,125	121,090
1943	961,545	160,060	382,537
1944	893,242	167,562	321,008
1945	941,733	117,334	92,733
1946	861,340	143,600	74,746
1947	684,441	215,679	31,400
1948	564,590	249,940	—
1949	517,459	267,869	—
1950	513,891	208,962	—
1951	315,275	133,823	—
1952	147,885	179,695	—
Total	10,904,020	2,774,234	1,117,421

Source: V. N. Zemskov, Ukaz. soch., p. 47.

accused of idleness and unauthorized departures; almost 1.8 million workers were sentenced to six months of corrective labor without reduction in normal work hours and were reduced to one-quarter pay, and 322,000 were imprisoned for from two to four months. In 1941, 3.2 million workers were subject to sanctions, and 633,000 served prison sentences. Both serious and petty offenders were susceptible to the arbitrary decisions of their superiors, who were authorized to punish virtually any action, such as the search for a better paying job or an apartment. Such harsh measures reduced labor turnover as intended. Immediately before the passage of the June 1940 law, labor turnover in ferrous metallurgy was 6.6 percent a month (4.2 percent were fired for idleness), but by the end of 1940, turnover fell to 1.9 percent a month.[8]

The Soviet system had its ways of moderating extreme laws. The implementation of draconian decrees depended on relationships in the work collective and on personal contacts. Enterprises found ways to sabotage laws that worked against their interests. Managers concealed absences and other violations if they felt it was in their interest.

THE WAR YEARS

The extraordinary measures and decrees put into effect in the period 1938–40 were suited to wartime. Combatant countries turned to more coercive labor measures (tying labor to factories, requiring longer hours, and so on) and appealed to patriotism. In the Soviet Union, coercive measures were particularly severe, and appeals to duty and patriotism were particularly vocal. Soviet authors emphasized patriotism as the rationale for immense sacrifices under the slogan "everything for the front, everything for victory" and saw the wartime emergency as fully justifying coercive methods. There is no dispute about the many acts of labor heroism during the war years, for example, the huge over-fulfillment of norms achieved "without sleep or rest" under the most difficult circumstances.[9] These wartime achievements may in fact have revealed the hidden reserves of the Soviet economy. Regardless of such individual acts of heroism, the war years saw a lowering of labor productivity on

8. Ibid.

9. It is necessary to mention among Western works that of John J. Barber and M. Harrison, *The Soviet Home Front, 1941–1945: A Social and Economic History of the USSR in World War II* (London: Longman, 1991). This book, based on Soviet sources, is free of ideological bias and covers many problems of work motivation during the war years.

a large scale as mobilized, qualified male workers were replaced by female and youth workers, and factories were evacuated to the east.

Stalin was not content to rely on patriotism but counted more on coercion and force, although the combination depended on the situation in the country and on the front. On November 30, 1941, the Committee for the Distribution of Labor was formed within the Council of People's Commissars to mobilize and redistribute labor resources. The February 1942 law of mobilization of men from age sixteen to fifty-five years and women from age sixteen to forty-five years brought some 12 million women and youth workers into factories and enterprises. The share of women in ferrous metals, a traditional male occupation, rose to 39 percent in 1945.[10] Some 2.1 million persons were subject to mobilization calls in schools of labor reserves. In 1941, about 826,000 were called; in 1943, about 771,000; in 1944, about 50,000; and in 1945, about 25,000.[11]

Rationing, which was reinstated at the start of the war, became more differentiated as the war progressed. A large number of norms for bread, meat, clothing, and shoes were established, with soldiers at the front receiving the highest norms. The norms of home-front workers depended on their priority. The lengthening of the workday and workweek meant that workers spent most of their time in the factory, where they were fed, provided with goods, and even slept. The 1945 volume of centralized consumer goods was thirteen times the prewar level.[12] The production of necessities fell and what was left over was reserved mainly for use at the front. Clothing, footwear, matches, kerosene, soap, and so forth, disappeared from state stores, and free market prices rose through the roof. Widespread corruption within the rationing system required the Defense Council to approve a decree on January 23, 1943, against the misuse of

10. *Rabochi Klass Nakanune i v Gody Veliko Otechestvennoy Voiny*, p. 353.
11. Ibid., 354.
12. Ibid., 407.

supplies in the official supply system, and special controllers were put in place whose activities were regulated by trade unions.

Most made do with what they had before the war. Rationing provided only minimal subsistence, but in besieged Leningrad supplies were considerably lower, and workers in Leningrad and elsewhere had to cover their minimal needs on the "free market." Accordingly, money wages maintained their value. In 1944, the average wage was 573 rubles a month, and in ferrous metals it rose as high as 697 rubles. In 1940 the premium share of compensation for engineering technical workers rose from 5 percent to 8 percent for workers and from 11 percent to 28 percent for engineering technical workers.[13]

On December 26, 1941, enterprises producing for the military were placed on a militarized regime. Unauthorized departures were judged not by People's Courts but by military judges. Absences from work and malicious idleness were considered as "deserting from the labor front" and could mean sentences in the Gulag of from five to eight years. Negligence leading to major accidents could be punished by execution. Punishment statistics (see Table 2.1) reveal that 121,090 workers were punished under the December 1941 law in 1942, 383,000 in 1943, and 93,000 in 1944. After the application of a military regime in transport in the spring of 1943, 50,000 transport workers were punished in the period 1943–44.[14] As the war moved toward its conclusion in late 1944, the number punished under these laws fell, and a decree of the Presidium of the Supreme Soviet of 30 December 1944 declared an amnesty for those who had left military factories if they voluntarily returned to their work. According to correspondence from Molotov to Stalin, some two hundred thousand "labor deserters" had been sentenced in absentia

13. Ibid., 405–406.
14. V. N. Zemskov, Ukaz. soch., p. 45.

and were on the loose.[15] Many of these deserters were young graduates of vocational schools, who justified their absence by the need to care for elderly parents or the family plot. To prove their case, they submitted letters from relatives, neighbors, and hospital officials. Many of these deserters were indeed working, only not at the place of employment designated by the state. Therefore, these punishment statistics do not reflect labor discipline in production but the priorities of state policy in allocating labor.

The principal legal basis for punishing violators of labor discipline remained the law of June 26, 1940, which besides imposing work sanctions and possible imprisonment reduced pay and food rations by 25 percent. In 1942, some 1.3 million workers were subject to these sanctions, and 297,000 were imprisoned from two to four months (see Table 2.1). In 1943 and 1944, some one million workers were punished each year, including some 160,000 who were imprisoned. In May of 1945, Germany was defeated, but sanctions continued to be imposed. Even after Germany's defeat, 942,000 workers were punished, including 117,000 who were imprisoned. Military laws also remained in force, and about 93,000 people were convicted according to the law of December 26, 1941 (see Table 2.1).

THE IMMEDIATE POSTWAR YEARS: REALITY VERSUS EXPECTATION

The aftermath of World War II was more difficult for the Soviet Union than for other countries. Its formerly occupied territories had been destroyed and turned into wastelands. The consequences of war were seen in the run-down capital stock as well as the deteriorating buildings. Reconstructing the economy and placing it on a civilian footing demanded substantial investments in the absence of

15. Ibid., 46.

economic reserves. More than 20 million people had been lost in the war, not counting the millions of war invalids and physically handicapped. The government had to establish orphanages and create pensions for the tens of millions of invalids and widows. The prewar social order had been torn apart by the loss of life, the millions of children without parents, and the deterioration in living standards. Social ties collapsed, and criminality and banditry were rampant. The population continued its wartime mentality, although the enemy had been vanquished, and the rhetoric of the cold war created the image of a new enemy, American imperialism. The armed forces continued to occupy a special position of authority. Society remained to a great extent mobilized, and the idea of a new peacetime society only slowly entered the consciousness of people. Many problems continued to be resolved by coercion and force, requiring an "iron hand" to restore order.

On the labor front, the Soviet Union emerged from the war with a wide gap between reality and expectations. Workers and their families felt that they deserved to live not only better than in the wartime years but also better than before the war. Such a feeling was particularly widespread among the 8 million soldiers and officers who were being demobilized to return to "peaceful and productive labor." Many were intent on careers other than hard labor in factories and collective farms, under the motto: "The people should decide which direction is better to take." For returning soldiers, the impression they had received of the higher living standards in Germany was overwhelming. Those who wanted to attend universities or to live in Moscow had to grapple with the internal passport system. Those who received official permission to live in Moscow were assigned to dormitories; others found places "in corridors" occupied by thieves, bandits, and the poor. In such an explosive situation, it was a blessing that few weapons remained in private hands.

The politics of labor in the postwar years was influenced by the public's dissatisfaction with living standards and working conditions, as shown by letters to political authorities and by questions asked during meetings and lectures.[16] A female worker in a Moscow plant wrote: "We worked hard throughout the war; we awaited the victory and counted on better conditions. The opposite occurred. They lowered our salaries and we receive pennies. It is time to think about the workers." Many letters sounded the leitmotiv: "Less chatter about the needs of workers, more about our real concerns." Collective farms were described as "souring organizations," from which all above-plan production was taken. And again: "Everybody is running away from the villages." Lecturers at factories in Moscow were asked: "How can you explain that German prisoners of war are receiving twice as much bread as those of us in need?" "Why is it that unemployed people in the West live better than we do who are working?" "What good is socialism when life is getting worse?" A letter to authorities reads: "My husband is an engineer. He gets 900 rubles per month and he cannot support a family of three. What does this say about workers with even larger families?" A letter, signed by Ivan the "son of a rat" (Ivan Krysovych) to emphasize his extreme poverty, complained that his application for boots had been turned down three times, and he promised to hang himself if turned down again. A female worker in Moscow was arrested for distributing a song titled the "Urban Toast" (a play on the famous "Village Toast"), which replaced "Be healthy, live a rich life" with "Be healthy, live a rich life / As much as is allowed by our salary / But if our salary does not allow you to live / Well no one is forcing you to

16. New documents from archives regarding this topic were included in the monograph of E. Yu. Zubkov, *Poslevoennoe Sovetskoe Obschestvo. 1945–1953 gg. Politika i Povsednevnost'* (Moscow, 1999). Many documents were published about postwar life, such as "Moskva Poslevoennaia. 1945–1947 gg. Arkhivnie Dokumenty i Materialy" (Moscow: Mosgorarkhiv 2000). Although the situation in Moscow had characteristics particular to metropolitan areas, the situation was common for the whole country.

survive." The attention of security organizations was attracted by one worker who, although earning eighteen hundred rubles a month, refused to buy obligatory state bonds, declaring: "When I am able to live well, then I'll sign up." Another worker wrote: "We are not lazy. We are working with all our might but they don't give us enough to live let alone to survive. It is not insulting when they reward scientists who are of value to society, but it is terrible when they give jazz singers the right to eat to their fill."[17] Although rationing remained in effect, workers complained that they had to buy all their goods in the market: "Commercial stores are full, but rationed goods are the worst products." "We can't even buy potatoes; what use are coupons?" Supply officials were accused of gluttony at the expense of workers' empty stomachs. Instances of large-scale corruption among supply officials were reported in large factories such as the Moscow Electrical Lamp Factory.[18] Two hundred vocational students in the Tagan region refused to eat in the school cafeteria, complaining that they could not eat one more bite of cabbage. "This is not a strike but a request to be fed."[19] An inspection revealed that the menu indeed consisted only of cabbage dishes.

The monetary reform of December 14, 1947, returned the economy to a more normal postwar footing. The old currency was exchanged for a new currency at the rate of ten to one, and only limited sums could be converted, thereby liquidating savings, such as those of a worker who had saved one thousand rubles to buy a coat.[20] Prices of rationed goods were raised close to those in commercial stores; fewer and fewer products were rationed, and the stimulus to work returned. According to one worker: "Under

17. Ibid., 111, 195, 277, 390.
18. Ibid., 390.
19. Ibid., 111.
20. Ibid., 277.

rationing, you bored yourself eating a few pieces of white bread; now you can eat until you are full."[21]

The public's clamor for a better life extended to demands for a better life in the workplace. Although the war had ended in the spring of 1945, the harsh labor laws of the late 1930s and war years remained on the books. Appeals for their repeal were common. Among the most "poisonous" questions posed at worker meetings were: "When will we be allowed to change freely from one enterprise to another?" "When are mobilized workers from other regions free to leave?" "Will the law about criminal punishments for tardiness be repealed?" "Is a new labor law in the works?" "Will the authorities penalize those workers who wish to work out of the home?" There were demands to "get rid of the laws and decrees that either directly or indirectly enslave our labor." Former soldiers who had been in Germany wrote: "There there is real freedom. But our workers did not fight for freedom for themselves but for oppression." One worker expressed himself as follows: "I want to work. I want to go to another factory as a sign of protest against Soviet serfdom. Give the worker free labor."[22]

Notwithstanding the public mood, Stalin's labor policy remained contradictory. The Council of People's Commissars decree of June 21, 1945, eliminated the lengthened workday and multiple shifts but also reduced the bonuses for plan overfulfillment that had allowed technical workers to earn two to three times their base salary. As the economy shifted to peacetime, production fell in factories not suited to civilian products, and workers complained of falling wages, lack of work, and irregular payments."[23] Mobilization as a source of labor began to erode. In May of 1946, about 203,000 mobilized, repatriated, and evacuated workers worked in

21. Ibid.
22. Ibid., 111–112.
23. Ibid., 380.

ferrous metallurgy, constituting 25 percent of its labor force; 10 percent of those were mobilized from vocational schools, and 6 percent were Gulag inmates. By the end of 1947, the share of mobilized workers in ferrous metallurgy fell to 14 percent, while the share of "nonmobilized" labor rose from 59 to 72 percent.[24] In 1946, some 1.5 million workers were supplied to enterprises and construction sites by organized recruitment, which was especially prominent among demobilized soldiers. But by May of 1947, organized recruitment was transferred to the ministry of labor reserves, and only four hundred thousand workers were recruited by this means. In March of 1955, the Presidium of the Supreme Soviet eliminated mobilization and organized recruitment as a way of organizing the labor force, but the organized placement of graduates continued. In the period 1946–50, 3.4 million young people acquired specialized training in specialized schools and were placed in enterprises for obligatory terms. Disappointed by their work, they found ways to extricate themselves from their obligations. The premature turnover of graduates was severe enough to warrant the Decree of August 2, 1948, which put in place measures to battle the turnover of graduates of vocational schools.

The strict labor laws of the war years were retained in the first years of the postwar period. Moscow and Leningrad factories were removed from wartime regulations in March of 1947, and the regulations were then dropped from factories in other territories in July of 1948, but the draconian law of June 1940 remained in effect (see Table 2.1). Turnover remained the scourge of Soviet employers, despite the fact that the antiturnover decrees remained intact. Turnover peaked in 1947, when it reached 64 percent of workers per year in construction, 54 percent in coal mining, 40 percent in the oil industry, 36 percent in metallurgy, and 34 percent in light industry. Difficult work and living conditions promoted labor turnover,

---

24. *Promyshlennost' i Rabochiy Klass SSSR*, p. 220.

which accelerated during the famine of 1946–47. The postwar displacements and continued high turnover rates even called forth a temporary harshening of criminal punishments. In 1949, almost a quarter million workers were subject to criminal punishment for unauthorized absences, laziness, and idleness; however, the number of fines fell during the same period by half.[25]

Appeals from workers, from their superiors, and from judicial workers finally led to the decree of the Presidium of the Supreme Soviet of July 14, 1951, "About the replacement of judicial responsibility of workers and employees for idleness, except in the case of multiple and extended absences with disciplinary and social actions," which reduced the number punished under the June 26, 1940, law to 180,000 (as compared to hundreds of thousands earlier).[26] In April of 1956 the law was dropped entirely. With the passage of the April 1956 law, the post-Stalin leadership turned decisively from "sticks" to "carrots" in the workforce as the harsh work laws of the period 1938 to 1940 faded into memory.

The rampant criminality of the early postwar years turned the attention of authorities from work discipline to theft of personal and state property. A campaign against the burgeoning postwar criminality and theft was initiated by two laws of June 4, 1947, that strengthened the protection of personal and social property. Convictions carried terms of five to six years for the theft of personal property, ten to fifteen years for banditry, seven to ten years for theft of state property, and ten to twelve years for group thefts. Punishments for nonreporting of crimes were set at two to three years. In the course of the campaign against theft, hundreds of thousands of people were sentenced, and for crimes committed earlier, sentences were raised. Chapters 1 and 4 reveal that almost

25. V. N. Zemskov, Ukaz. soch., p. 45.
26. Ibid.

a million inmates of the Gulag were sentenced under anticrime laws in the early 1950s.

THE GULAG

This chapter has focused mainly on the "civilian" labor force of the Soviet Union, which constituted around 95 million people in 1950. It has said little about inmates of the Soviet Gulag, working in camps and colonies under harsh climatic conditions in remote areas, typically for no pay. Although other chapters deal extensively with the Gulag, we focus here on only a few points. Gulag labor, like "civilian labor," underwent changes in the war years. At the war's beginning, a number of large Gulag projects were wrapped up, and other projects were cut back. Many inmates were freed and dispatched to the front; others were sent into penal battalions. Many inmates also went voluntarily to the front, spurred by patriotic enthusiasm. Accordingly, the number of inmates in the Gulag system fell considerably. This reduction in numbers was supposed to be compensated for by a doubling of norms for those remaining. The workday was extended. Sickness and mortality rose because of increased work and worsening provisions. New forms of forced labor, such as labor worker columns and military construction units similar to those used during the civil war, were introduced.

Gulag administrators of penal labor, like their civilian counterparts, realized over time that coercion alone did not produce high labor productivity. To raise the effectiveness of Gulag labor required material incentive schemes and investments of scarce capital resources. The Gulag was at first expected to be a "magic wand" that would build major projects in short order, such as the White Sea–Baltic Canal in 1931 (see Chapters 8 and 9). However, it was discovered that the Gulag required equipment, skilled labor, experienced specialists, and better worker qualifications, all of which raised the cost of maintaining the Gulag. Labor productivity in the

Gulag's production administrations was only 50 to 60 percent of comparable civilian administrations. Economic methods for raising the motivation of prisoners began to be introduced. In November of 1948, the Council of Ministers decreed that Gulag workers were to receive wages, but only 30 percent of what workers in corresponding civilian branches received.[27] Gulag wages were composed mainly of bonuses and piece-rate payments. In the economic branches of the Gulag, tariffs and norms for the payment of labor were gradually raised throughout the postwar period, and an eight-hour day was eventually established. By 1953, paid contingents in camps constituted 62 percent.[28] Those not paid included invalids, those refusing to work, and a few other classes of prisoners. The average monthly pay of prisoners was 324 rubles a month, of which they received 129 rubles after charges for their maintenance.[29] Perhaps even more important, a system of accounts *(zachet)* was restored for more than half of Gulag inmates by which prison sentences were reduced according to the number of days of overfulfillment of norms. Measures to raise labor productivity were generally not successful, although the term reductions for good work were considered effective. In the period 1951–52, not one production administration of the Gulag fulfilled its plan for raising labor productivity.[30] And the 1953 plan was characterized as unsatisfactory.[31]

The 2.5 million prisoners of war in Soviet camps in 1946 did not provide a great boost to production. Foreigners could not survive the Soviet Gulag. They were often sick, had high rates of mor-

27. The newest publication of Gulag documents, including the third volume, shows that this decree provoked a series of normative acts that set the rate of prisoners' wages in individual camps and in the different industries of the Gulag economy.

28. *Gulag. 1918–1960* (Moscow, 2000), p. 667.

29. Ibid., 669.

30. *Sistema Ispravitel'no-Trudovykh Lagerey v SSSR, 1923–1960* (Moscow, 1998), p. 49.

31. *Gulag*, p. 670.

tality, and showed little interest in work. International pressure also required that they be maintained at a higher standard of living than Soviet inmates were. Prisoners of war constituted a headache for the camp administration; and Soviet authorities attempted to rid themselves as quickly as possible of foreign prisoners of war. By 1949 there were only ten thousand such prisoners remaining, primarily those convicted of war crimes.

The Gulag experienced its apogee in the early postwar period. The number of Gulag inmates rose to 2.5 million in 1950.[32] In the aftermath of war, camps filled with deserters, military criminals, collaborators with occupation forces, participants in national movements, and other real or imagined anti-Soviet elements. Half the inmate population was composed of those sentenced under the June 1940 law. The Gulag administration saw wisdom in separating political from criminal prisoners and created special camps for political prisoners. Camps were differentiated by security regimes. According to the decree about "working zones," the strictest regime with the highest security was reserved for the most dangerous criminals, but the equipment for strict security was deficient. Other prisoners worked without guards. Prisoners working without guards rose to 11 percent of all inmates in 1947 and continued to grow after that.

On the initiative of the minister of interior, L. P. Beria, the liquidation of the Gulag occurred quickly after Stalin's death in March of 1953. As someone who had been involved in the system for a long time, Beria was more aware of the real situation of forced labor, its ineffectiveness, its low labor productivity, and the unprofitability of colonies. Large gulag projects were first to be closed; the production administrations were abandoned; and a group of camps was closed down. On March 27, 1953, amnesty was declared

32. V. N. Zemskov, "Gulag (Istoriko-Sotsiologicheskiy Aspekt)," *SOTsIS,* 1991, No. 6, p. 13. Some experts add about three hundred thousand convicts plus those in transit.

for those with sentences of up to five years. Beria called for an examination of all criminal legislation, replaced the "special meeting" of the MVD, and began an examination of "political cases." Beria's arrest and execution inhibited these initiatives, but after a while the liquidation of the Gulag system was resumed, accelerated by Gulag uprisings in 1953 and 1954.[33] In 1954 the examination of political cases began, and in 1955 those who collaborated with occupying forces were granted amnesty. Declarations of amnesty for political prisoners accelerated after the Twentieth Party Congress, in which Khrushchev delivered his secret speech against Stalin's crimes, and the history of the camps came to an end in October of 1959. A joint decree of the Central Committee and Council of Ministers closed down the Gulag for not fulfilling its primary function, "the rehabilitation of prisoners by means of labor." At this time, 948,000 people were incarcerated, of which only 1.2 percent had been sentenced for anti-Soviet crimes.[34] Most special camps were liquidated, and labor colonies were turned over to local offices of the MVD.

Thus by the mid-1950s, coercion in the Soviet workplace—ranging from harsh penalties for relatively minor infractions to the extreme coercion of the Gulag—had been largely abandoned. The rejection of force was not related to particular personalities but to the inherent ineffectiveness of force in the workplace. Even Beria, one of the most ardent advocates of coercion, had concluded that it did not work. Any other administrator working in these circumstances would have favored a liberalization of the regime, since the punishment system had worn itself out, and a new means of motivating labor had to be found in the 1960s.

33. There is a substantial body of literature on camp revolts. For official reports, see reference note 32. It should be noted that the rebels advocated labor rights equal to those of "free" workers.

34. V. N. Zemskov, Ukaz. soch., p. 15.

The Economy of the OGPU, NKVD, and MVD of the USSR, 1930–1953

The Scale, Structure, and Trends of Development

Oleg Khlevnyuk

THE AMOUNT OF research done on issues of forced labor in the USSR has been meager, and this becomes a problem when we attempt to outline the range of forced labor institutions and facilities. Historians focus most often on enterprises and construction projects managed directly by the OGPU, NKVD, and MVD. But a certain portion of prisoners, special settlers, prisoners of war, and others who were under the administration of the OGPU, NKVD, and MVD were sent to work for other ministries as well. In addition, millions of people were sentenced to correctional labor and mostly served the sentences at their places of employment. Finally, there were forced-labor institutions for individuals who were nominally free. One example was the so-called *tyloopolchentsy* (logistical guardsmen) during the 1930s.[1] We will add to this list as we delve deeper into the problem and uncover the different kinds and forms of forced labor in the Stalinist system. But it is hardly debatable that the nucleus and most significant part of the forced-labor economy was the economy controlled by the Soviet

---

1. S. A. Krasilnikov and D. D. Minenkov, "Tylovoye Opolcheniye kak Element Sistemy Prinuditelnogo Truda: Etap Stanovleniya (1930–1933 gg.)" in *Gumanitarnye Nauki v Sibiri*, 2001, No. 2, pp. 41–46.

punitive bodies—the OGPU, NKVD, and MVD. The development of this sector of the economy is the subject of this chapter.

The period defined in the title covers the years in which the Stalinist version of the forced-labor economy took shape and proliferated. While prisoner labor was used on a fairly wide scale both in prerevolutionary Russia and during the early postrevolutionary years, the fundamentally new system of the Gulag economy didn't emerge until the end of the 1920s and beginning of the 1930s, as a result of the policy of the great industrial leap forward, forced collectivization, and the mass repressions that accompanied them. This economy was typified by huge projects whose construction and operation required the large-scale use of unskilled workers, as a rule, in regions that were hard to reach, that had an extremely unfavorable climate, and that lacked a basic infrastructure. Relentless exploitation of prisoners in hard physical work, mainly in construction, mining, and logging, was the essence of the Stalinist version of the forced-labor economy.

The events that immediately followed Stalin's death in 1953 suggested that this economy was being dismantled (if not completely, then at least substantially). On the one hand, a mass amnesty and the subsequent rehabilitations significantly reduced the number of prisoners. On the other, many costly projects that were under construction by prisoners were scrapped, and the MVD lost many production functions as it transferred most of its enterprises to economic ministries. While this process was an erratic one and was marked by backsliding, the overall trend of dismantling the MVD economy in its Stalinist form continued. A gradual transition was under way from a system of camps that served as a source of unskilled workers to a system of correctional labor colonies that had their own production base. This stage of the evolution of the camp economy after Stalin's death requires special scrutiny.

This chapter, based mostly on the archives and available literature,[2] has two main objectives: first, to sketch a general picture of the development of the OGPU-NKVD-MVD economy and its quantitative parameters, and second, to outline several approaches to studying the important but extremely complex problem of the efficiency of the Gulag economy and the role of forced labor in the industrial development of the USSR.

To some degree we can trace the starting point of the Stalinist Gulag and its economy to the Politburo resolution of June 27, 1929, "On the Use of the Labor of Convicted Criminals." To supplement the Solovetsky camp, which was the only one at the time, the resolution directed that a network of new camps be created in the country's remote areas to colonize them and develop "natural resources by using prisoner labor."[3] At first the intention was to set up small camps—with a total capacity of up to fifty thousand inmates. But the tremendous wave of terror associated with a radical turnaround in policy, the so-called dekulakization, and the forcible creation of collective farms substantially changed these plans. Several thousand peasants were arrested and exiled in a few months. At the same time that so-called special settlements for kulaks were being established, there was a sharp rise in the number of inmates

2. D. J. Dallin and B. P. Nicolaevsky, *Forced Labor in Soviet Russia* (New Haven: Yale University Press, 1947); N. Jasny, "Labour and Output in Soviet Concentration Camps," *The Journal of Political Economy* 59 (October 1951): 405–19; S. Swianiewicz, *Forced Labour and Economic Development. An Enquiry into the Experience of Soviet Industrialization* (London: 1965); O. P. Yelantseva, *Obrechonnaya Doroga. BAM: 1932–1941* (Vladivostok, 1994); M. Kraveri and O. Khlevnyuk "Krizis Ekonomiki MVD (konets 1940-x–1950-e gody)" in *Cahiers du Monde Russe*, XXXVI (1–2), 1995, pp. 179–190; *Ekonomika Gulaga i ego Rol' v Razvitii Strany. 1930-e gody. Sbornik Dokumentov.* Compiled by M. I. Khlusov (Moscow, 1998); L. I. Gvozdkova (ed.), *Prinuditelny Trud. Ispravitelno-Trudovyye Lagerya v Kuzbasse (30-50-e gody).* Vols. 1–2 (Kemerovo, 1994); A. I. Shirikov, *Dalstroi: Predistoriya i Pervoye Desyatiletiye* (Magadan, 2000); *GULAG (Glavnoye Upravleniye Lagerei). 1917–1960 gg.* Compiled by A. I. Kokurin and N. V. Petrov (Moscow, 2000); and others.

3. Russian State Archive of Social and Political History (hereafter—RGASPI) 17.3.746: 2, 11.

in newly created camps—almost 180,000 on January 1, 1930, which was several times more than the limits that had been set just six months earlier.

The OGPU leadership now faced the problem of making economic use of these several hundred thousand inmates and special settlers. At first, they had no coherent plans in this regard. Exiled peasants were turned over to work at other ministries' enterprises, mostly for logging. Camp inmates were used for different construction projects and in the timber industry. Often camps entered into their own agreements with enterprises and supplied them with labor.

The development of the OGPU economy was strongly influenced by the decision to build the White Sea–Baltic Canal (BBK). Construction of this transportation system, which started in the second half of 1930, was completed in record time—two years. At times more than one hundred thousand prisoners were used in the construction. For the first time, the camp economy demonstrated its "advantages" in practice: rapid deployment of worker contingents to a site and the ability to exploit prisoners in any conditions, regardless of casualties. Methods of organizing the Gulag's large economic projects were refined at the BBK as the Chekist leadership gained experience. After the BBK, the OGPU began to establish other major economic divisions. On November 11, 1931, the Politburo adopted a decision to form a special trust, later named Dalstroi (Far North Construction), "to speed up the development of gold mining in the upper reaches of the Kolyma."[4] On September 30, 1932, the Politburo adopted a decision to turn over to the OGPU the construction of a canal linking the Volga with the Moskva River, and on October 23, the construction of the Baikal-Amur Railroad in the Far East (BAM).[5] In October 1932, the OGPU also formed

4. RGASPI 17.162.11: 57.
5. RGASPI 17.3.902: 8; 904: 6, 46–52.

the Ukhta-Pechora Trust to organize coal and oil production and to develop other resources in the Pechora Basin.[6]

These decisions shaped the structure of the Gulag's economy, which existed and developed right up until the mid-1950s. The nucleus of this system was large construction projects and mining complexes that required massive use of unskilled labor in extreme conditions. By the beginning of 1935, more than 150,000 camp inmates were building the BAM, and 196,000 were working on the Moskva-Volga Canal. The White Sea–Baltic project—the system of transport and industrial enterprises concentrated around the BBK— employed 71,000 inmates. A total of 21,000 inmates from the Ukhta-Pechora camp were extracting oil and coal. The Far Eastern camps (60,000 inmates) were mining coal, building railroads and a shipyard in Komsomolsk-on-Amur, and so on. The 63,000 inmates from the Siberian camp were building railroads and carrying out projects for metallurgical and other enterprises. At the Svir camp, 43,000 inmates were procuring lumber and firewood for Leningrad; at the Temnikovo camp 35,000 inmates were performing similar jobs for Moscow. The Karaganda and Central Asian camps (about 26,000 inmates each) specialized in agriculture, but they also supported industrial enterprises and construction projects.[7] In the mid-1930s the Dalstroi trust (36,000 inmates in January 1935) was rapidly building up the mining of gold. In the first six years of operation (1928–33), 1,937 kg of gold was obtained on the Kolyma. In 1934 a large leap occurred, and from 1934 to 1936, Dalstroi produced more than 53 tons of gold. In 1937, Dalstroi produced 51.5 tons.[8]

The situation on the Kolyma reflected the general state of the

6. RGASPI 17.3.904: 10; 906: 40–44.

7. State Archive of Russian Federation (hereafter—GARF) R-5446.16a.1310: 13–14.

8. GARF-R. 5446.17.278: 75; 20a.949b: 2; 984: 2; A. I. Shirokov, *Dalstroi*, p. 103.

NKVD economy in the mid-1930s. After an extremely severe crisis in 1932 and 1933, marked by mass famine and mortality in the Gulag (as well as throughout the country), the system stabilized. While prisoner population growth was insignificant, there was an increase in production and large projects carried out by camps. In June 1935 the Gulag was assigned the priority construction of the Norilsk Nickel Integrated Plant. The NKVD used substantial capital investments in carrying out construction projects for the Committee on Reserves (such as warehouses for storage of reserve state stocks of foodstuffs and industrial goods).

The relatively successful development of the forced-labor economy was interrupted by the Great Terror—the mass repressions of 1937 and 1938. Between January 1, 1937, and January 1, 1939, the population of camps and colonies rose from 1.2 million to nearly 1.7 million. On January 1, 1939, there were 350,000 people in prisons, and about one million people were living in labor settlements.[9] But in spite of the formidable increase in the prisoner population, the Gulag economy was going through a severe crisis. The NKVD leadership, preoccupied with carrying out mass repressions, was not interested in economic problems. Enterprises under the NKVD authority were disorganized by the arrests of their directors, by mass executions, and by the sharp increase in the mortality rate and the physical exhaustion of camp inmates. The plans for capital construction and industrial production were not being fulfilled.

The situation that resulted from the Great Terror in the Gulag showed that the political motives for the Terror took absolute priority over economic ones. The crowded camps and the impossibility of putting the hundreds of thousands of new prisoners to work explain the unprecedented number of death sentences—between August 1937 and November 1938, according to official data, almost

---

9. V. N. Zemskov, "Gulag (Istoriko-Sotsiologichesky Aspect)" in *Sotsis*, 1991, No. 6, p. 11.

seven hundred thousand people were executed.[10] A significant part of them, a list of those executed shows,[11] were able-bodied men, highly qualified specialists and workers, who were constantly in short supply at NKVD projects. The main purpose of the Great Terror was declared at the very outset to be the physical annihilation of "enemies" rather than their use as "cheap" labor.

The NKVD economy stabilized somewhat and then grew between 1939 and early 1941 as the Terror abated. Economic growth was achieved through the "utilization of internal reserves"—intensified exploitation of prisoners, some adjustments in the management of camps, and so on. To this end, the new USSR people's commissar of internal affairs, Lavrenty Beria, carried out administrative "reforms" in the spring and summer of 1939. Their purpose was to eliminate so-called workday credits, which had reduced the convict's sentence by a certain proportion of the time worked in production. The elimination of this system allowed worker contingents to stabilize but brought about the destruction of the last quasi-economic incentives in the NKVD economy. The elimination of "credits," which had been the most effective way of motivating prisoner labor, was accompanied by tougher repressions (up to and including execution) against the "disorganizers" of camp production.[12]

After World War II began in 1939, the Soviet government feverishly and hurriedly adopted resolutions on the construction of military enterprises and facilities. Most of these plans were assigned to the NKVD. The most massive project during this period was the railroad construction in the Far East and the northern part of the European USSR. The NKVD hydraulic-engineering projects

10. *GULAG (Glavnoye Upravleniye Lagerei), 1917–1960 gg.*, pp. 433.
11. See the many memorial books and martyrologies issued in recent years in almost every region of Russia as well as M. Ilic, "The Great Terror in Leningrad: A Quantitative Analysis," *Europe-Asia Studies* 52, no. 8 (2000): 1515–1534.
12. GARF. R-5446.23a.76: 6–9; 121: 6–9; R-9414.1.1152: 2–4.

accounted for the second-largest volume: canals (the Volga-Baltic and Northern Dvina waterways, which linked the Baltic Sea and the White Sea with the Caspian Sea), hydroelectric stations, and ports. The NKVD's nonferrous metal production surged sharply during the prewar years: there were increases in the production of gold, nickel (Norilsk Integrated Plant and the Severonikel [Northern Nickel] Integrated Plant in Murmansk Province), tin and copper (Dzhezkazgan Integrated Plant). The NKVD played a substantial role in the program, adopted in October 1940, to raise aluminum and magnesium production.

Prisoners set up a new oil installation in the European North and built hydrolysis, sulfite-liquor, and aircraft plants, roads, and many other facilities. In 1940 the NKVD's capital investments amounted to 14 percent of total centralized capital investments.[13] An extremely intensive construction plan was approved for 1941 as well. The transfer of new industrial enterprises and construction projects to the NKVD continued right up to the German invasion in June 1941. The most significant assignment, received by the people's commissariat on March 24, 1941, was to build and renovate 251 airfields for the People's Commissariat of Defense in 1941. To carry out this assignment, the NKVD had to allocate four hundred thousand prisoners, and the People's Commissariat of Defense had to form one hundred construction battalions of one thousand men each.

While many NKVD assignments during the prewar period were already of value for military mobilization, the outbreak of war caused substantial adjustments in the economic activities of the people's commissariat. The development of the NKVD economy during the war was influenced by several important factors. There were quantitative and qualitative changes in the worker contingents managed by the NKVD. Because some camps and colonies had to

13. GARF R-5446.25a.7181: 35–36.

be evacuated, and conditions in the Gulag deteriorated in 1941, about 420,000 inmates were given an early release. In 1942 and 1943, about 157,000 inmates who had been convicted of minor offenses were given early releases and turned over to the army.[14] The mortality rate in the Gulag during the war was extremely high. From 1941 through 1945, according to ministry statistics, 1,005,000 inmates died in camps and colonies.[15] As a result, despite an influx of new inmates, their total number declined considerably. Between July 1, 1941, and February 11, 1945, for example, the population in the camps and colonies dropped from 2.3 million to 1.4 million. Moreover, a high percentage of inmates were sick and exhausted. Even according to official data, the share of camp inmates working in production declined between 1942 and 1944 to 65 to 70 percent, and the share of sick inmates rose to about 20 percent.[16] The prisoner shortage was somewhat offset by the so-called mobilized contingents—400,000 Soviet citizens with ethnic backgrounds from countries that were at war with the USSR (Germans, Finns, Romanians). Some 220,000 of them were sent to NKVD economic facilities, while the rest were turned over to other people's commissariats.[17] Some were housed in camps on the same footing as prisoners. During the last period of the war, prisoners of war, contingents from screening and interrogation camps, and so forth, were increasingly used for labor.

The small amount of fully capable workers, along with such factors as the mass evacuation of many facilities and the war-mobilization restructuring of the economy, had an effect on the scale and structure of the NKVD's economic activities. Although the NKVD of the USSR remained one of the most important construction agen-

14. GULAG (Glavnoye Upravleniye Lagerei), 1917–1960 gg., p. 275.
15. A. Kokurin, and Yu. Morukov "GULAG: Struktura i Kadry" in Svobodnaya Mysl', 2000, No. 10, p. 118.
16. GARF R-9414.1.330: 56–61.
17. GULAG (Glavnoye Upravleniye Lagerei), 1917–1960 gg., p. 281.

cies, the total amount of capital construction (at least in relation to cost) declined significantly. At the same time the structure of capital investments changed substantially. The share of railroad, road, and especially hydraulic-engineering construction declined from the pre-war period. Meanwhile, the role of the people's commissariat increased in the construction of enterprises for the steel industry, the nonferrous metal industry, the fuel industry, and airfield construction.[18] Military needs required the conversion of many NKVD industrial enterprises to the production of ammunition, uniforms, and so on.[19]

The smaller number of prisoners during the war, the postwar amnesty, and the release of several classes of prisoners who had been detained at the NKVD facilities until the war ended, substantially lowered the capability of the NKVD economy. According to estimates by the NKVD itself, the total worker shortfall at its enterprises for the second half of 1945 was 750,000 men.[20] The people's commissariat leadership also took a rather skeptical view in late 1945 and early 1946 of the economic prospects of the NKVD ministry. This skepticism fully manifested itself when the NKVD drew up plan goals for the fourth Five-Year Plan (1946–50), which provided for a reduction in prisoner labor and a commensurate reduction in the plans.[21]

An increase in repressions, however, actually caused the number of prisoners to rise after the war. As a result, the MVD not only allocated a large number of prisoner workers to different economic people's commissariats but also continued to build up its own economic activities throughout the postwar period until the time of Stalin's death.

18. Calculation based on: GARF R-5446.50a.3888: 83–85.
19. *GULAG (Glavnoye Upravleniye Lagerei), 1917–1960 gg.*, pp. 289–294.
20. GARF R-9401.1.2204: 118.
21. GARF R-9401.1.2209: 106–109; R-5446.48a.2465: 62–66.

A substantial role was played in research and development by several kinds of MVD design bureaus (*sharashki*), whose activities are very difficult to research because of the inaccessibility of documents.

The MVD remained the largest construction ministry. The prewar structure of MVD capital projects, which favored mining and infrastructure projects, was largely restored after the war. This restoration was caused, on the one hand, by a halt to the construction of steel-industry enterprises and airfields during the war, and on the other hand, by the MVD's greater participation in railroad, and especially hydraulic-engineering, construction. Beginning in 1950, prisoners built numerous hydraulic facilities, which official propaganda dubbed "Stalin's construction projects of communism": the Volga-Don, Volga-Baltic, and Turkmen Canals and the Kuibyshev and Stalingrad hydroelectric stations. Military-industrial facilities held a special place in the MVD economy, above that of all atomic-energy industry projects. The share of these "special construction projects" in the total volume of capital construction by the MVD during the decisive period of the atomic project's implementation (1947–48) rose from 24.6 to 30.5 percent, though in 1949 the share fell to 21.3 percent.[22]

The amount of capital construction performed by the MVD roughly doubled from 1949 to 1952, reaching about 9 percent of total state capital investments in 1952.[23] In large measure this rapid pace was because of the overall economic policy, marked during the last years of Stalin's life by an acceleration of capital construction and investment in heavy industry, mainly in military sectors. The big jump in capital projects, as usual, overheated the economy

22. Calculation based on GARF R-5446.50a.3888: 83–85; R-9401.2.234: 15; R-5446. 80a.7595: 8–9; R-9414.1.326: 30.

23. Russian State Archive of the Economy (hereafter—RGAE) 1562.33.250: 64–65; 41.52: 67, 94–95.

and intensified its recessionary tendencies, leading, for example, to the immobilization of resources in unfinished construction. This policy exacerbated budget problems and contributed to the further decline of agriculture and the social sector. The recession in the MVD economy was a specific instance of the general crisis. The estimated cost of projects included in MVD plans for 1953 was 105 billion rubles, though the plan for MVD capital projects for that year was 13.3 billion rubles.[24] The only solution to this situation, as well as to the overfunding of capital construction as a whole, was to scrap some projects and cut capital investments.

Shortly after Stalin's death, on March 17, 1953, Lavrenty Beria, who had taken over the new Ministry of Internal Affairs, which had merged with the MGB (Ministry of State Security), sent the Presidium of the Communist Party Central Committee a memorandum addressed to Georgy Malenkov. Because of this memorandum the government adopted a resolution the next day to transfer all construction and industrial enterprises from the MVD to the economic ministries. (A decision to transfer the MVD's agriculture was adopted in May.) At the same time, on Beria's instructions, the MVD prepared proposals for a substantial cutback in its construction program. Large construction projects with an estimated cost of 49 billion rubles were to be shut down (out of a total estimated cost for all MVD construction projects of 105 billion). Meanwhile, the plan for capital projects at other facilities for 1953 declined from 13.3 billion to about 10 billion rubles. On March 21, Beria sent the relevant draft resolution to the Council of Ministers, and it was soon approved. Then came a decision to issue a broad amnesty and to release about 1 million of the 2.5 million prisoners. This reorganization concluded with a USSR Council of Ministers reso-

24. *GULAG (Glavnoye Upravleniye Lagerei), 1917–1960 gg.*, pp. 788–789.

lution on March 28, 1953, to transfer the camps and colonies (except special camps) from the MVD to the Ministry of Justice.[25]

Of course, the overextension of capital projects was only one cause (albeit an important one) of the crisis of the Stalinist Gulag and of the decisions adopted in 1953. The political element of the crisis, which also influenced the forced-labor economy, consisted of unrest in the camps, an increase in "camp banditry," and so on. There is also evidence indicating that the inefficiency of the forced-labor economic system was already obvious while Stalin was alive and that the leadership of the MVD and the government were aware of it.

One of the severest problems was the issue of incentives for prisoner labor. Although there was a strict legislative ban on the use of "workday credits," which had been eliminated in 1939, the MVD leadership claimed that credits were the most effective way of rewarding prisoner labor, and it sought after the war to reinstate this system at certain projects. As a result, by September 1950 "workday credits" were in use at camps housing more than 27 percent of all prisoners,[26] and the process was on the upswing. Although the proliferation of "credits" intensified the shortage of labor from the camps, the MVD leaders preferred this course, acknowledging, in effect, the inefficiency of administrative punitive measures.

Readiness for gradual change in the Gulag was shown by the MVD support of campaigns for the early release of prisoners followed by their assignment to enterprises as free workers. In August 1950, because of the relevant government resolution, the minister of internal affairs issued an order for the early release of eight thousand prisoners and their assignment to build railroads.[27] In

25. Ibid., 786–793.
26. GARF R-5446.80.7561: 40–43.
27. GARF R-9414.1.1363: 10.

January 1951, Internal Affairs Minister Sergei Kruglov requested that Beria authorize the early release of six thousand prisoners, who would then be transferred as free workers to the construction of the Kuibyshev and Stalingrad hydroelectric stations. Kruglov based this request on the lack of skilled workers to operate the machinery at these projects.[28] In February 1951 the Council of Ministers approved the MVD's proposals for the early release of a group of prisoners and their use "for the purpose of increasing permanent worker cadres" in the Pechora coal basin.[29] Consequently, despite the apparent advantages of unlimited control of prisoners, the authorities increasingly preferred to deal with relatively free workers, who provided higher labor productivity and did not require a well-oiled system of guards and overseers. Because of these measures and the transfer to the MVD's authority of new industries from other ministries, the proportion of free workers at MVD projects increased. In the first half of 1950 the total number of free workers in the MVD's basic production and capital construction (excluding the free members of camp management) was 662,000, or 38.9 percent of all those employed; free workers numbered 372,000, or 28.6 percent.[30]

One reason for the gradual reorientation of the MVD economy toward skilled free workers was the change in the methods of work at the ministry's projects. For example, mechanized timber haulage under the NKVD-MVD made up 23.9 percent of total timber haulage in 1939 and rose to 41.1 percent in 1947 and 53.6 percent in 1950. The share of mechanized timber cutting (with power saws) rose from 19.6 to 41.7 percent.[31] The number of excavators at construction projects of the NKVD-MVD was 158 at the beginning

28. GARF R-5446.86a.7384: 26–27.
29. GARF R-5446.81b.6557: 83–84, 124.
30. GARF R-9401.1.3586: 61–62.
31. GARF R-5446.24a.2940: 2–3; 50a.4111: 159; 81b.6512: 118.

of 1940 and 955 at the end of 1952.[32] At the same time, the machinery was becoming more refined and powerful. The mechanization of earth-moving operations increased between 1946 and 1952 from 52 to 87.8 percent.[33]

To raise the labor productivity of prisoners, the MVD leadership also sought, starting at the end of 1940, to convert certain camps to a wage system, thereby violating one of the principles of the forced-labor economy—its total lack of remuneration. On March 13, 1950, yielding to the MVD's persistent demands, the government adopted a resolution to introduce wages for prisoners at all correctional-labor camps and colonies, except special camps, which housed "especially dangerous" common and political criminals.[34] Soon after that, wages were also introduced at special camps.

Economic expediency made it constantly necessary to break the strict rules of prisoner confinement. The practice was widespread, for example, of so-called *raskonvoirovaniye* (removing escorts)— or releasing prisoners from the surveillance of guards and allowing prisoners to move relatively freely outside camp zones. Since camp administrators weren't able to provide guards in the production process, camp administrators either sought official permission for *raskonvoirovaniye* or introduced it without permission but with the center's tacit acquiescence.

These and similar occurrences pointed to a postwar trend in the MVD economy of converting prisoners to partly free employees— roughly a conversion of slaves to serfs. Further development of this process inevitably resulted in a fundamental reorganization of the Gulag, especially since the MVD economy faced mounting problems on the eve of Stalin's death, despite the attempts at limited

32. *GULAG (Glavnoye Upravleniye Lagerei), 1917–1960 gg.*, p. 778; RGAE 1562.33.1531: 101–102.

33. GARF R-9401.1.2641: 384; RGAE 1562.33.1531: 100.

34. GARF R-5446.80a.7641: 51-54.

"reforms" mentioned earlier. The share of prisoners used in production was declining. Labor productivity was dropping (26 to 28 percent of the prisoners employed in piecework failed to meet production targets in 1951–52).[35] Combined with the general economic crisis caused by the jump in capital investment in heavy industry, the recession in the camp economy itself made it much easier to adopt major political decisions in the spring of 1953.

The dismantling of the Stalinist forced-labor economy immediately after Stalin's death provides direct proof of its inexpediency and inefficiency but doesn't answer the question about the real role of that sector of the economy in Soviet industrialization. By the moral and legal criteria applied in civilized societies, the Stalinist terror and its derivative, the forced-labor economy, can only be classed as crimes. In the context of the larger trends of world development, which demonstrate the indisputable advantages of free labor, no forced-labor economy can be considered efficient. There is, however, another valid approach to this problem, which provisionally can be called a "historical" approach. It sets aside the factors mentioned above and evaluates the Stalinist forced-labor economy in the context of the realities of its time.

One such reality between the 1930s and 1950s was Soviet industrialization, which, as has been repeatedly pointed out in the literature, had the extensive task of catching up with the West. For that reason, the state pursued its objectives mainly by coercive methods. Based on this "historical" approach, some historians regard the Gulag economy as a necessary means of accelerating industrialization as a whole. Their view boils down to the following. Wide-scale use of "conventional" coercion and force in the economy (for example, emergency laws governing labor activities) had failed to accomplish tasks of accelerated industrialization. It was thus natural to create a large sector of absolutely forced labor, which by many

35. GARF R-9401.1.3821: 190.

standards was slave labor. While forced labor began because of political factors (mass political repressions), it later followed mostly an economic logic of development as the need for new workers provoked further repressions. In the opinion of such historians, the forced-labor economy performed the following functions, which were impossible (or nearly impossible) to carry out by the "conventional" methods of coercion and labor incentives.

First, it provided for the development of remote regions where attracting free workers required substantial funds. Second, it supplied extremely mobile labor, which was easily transferred from project to project in accord with the state's needs. Third, this labor could be exploited without restriction, to the point of complete exhaustion. Fourth, the threat of falling into the Gulag's maw served to "discipline" "free" workers. Fifth, the existence of a substantial population of prisoners and other "special contingents" relieved pressure on the meager consumer-goods market and made it easier to solve the most serious social problems (for example, housing), and so on. In sum, the use of prisoners was "a type of labor mobilization that was fully in line with the stage of extensive industrialization that ended in the 1950s."[36]

These factors are mainly of an a priori nature and have never been studied in concrete terms, using a broad range of sources. Moreover, it is obvious that such works will not appear any time soon and will require serious effort by many researchers. The new documents available, nevertheless, allow some initial observations and corrections to be made.

There are two fundamental points to be made. First, the view that the forced-labor economy and its deliberate expansion through

36. M. Van der Linden, "Forced Labour and Non-Capitalist Industrialization: The Case of Stalinism (c. 1929–c. 1956)," in *Free and Unfree Labour. The Debate Continues*, ed. T. Brass and M. Van der Linden (Berne, New York: Peter Lang, 1997), 351–362. This paper summarizes the main points of the debate.

terror were "necessary" was largely based on notions that there were an extremely large number of prisoners in the country. As one researcher wrote, for example, in 1940 and 1950 prisoners made up about 23 percent of all workers in the nonagrarian sector.[37] The archives, however, as the literature has repeatedly pointed out, provide much lower figures for the camp population. For example, in 1950 the camps, colonies, and prisons held an average of about 2.7 million inmates, while about 2.5 million were probably special settlers in exile.[38] A significant number of these 5.2 million, however, were disabled. For example, on January 1, 1950, about 2 million of the 2.5 million prisoners in the camps and colonies were able-bodied,[39] and the number of special settlers included members of their families. Since only a part of the able-bodied were employed in industrial sectors, the total number of prisoners and "special contingents" sent to industry and construction in 1950 was probably not much higher than 2 million. Meanwhile, the total number of people employed in industry and construction in 1950 was 18.6 million (this number probably did not include prisoners).

To comprehend the real role that the Gulag played in the industrialization of the USSR, we must, above all, ask what kinds of work the prisoners were employed in. At first glance (although this question also requires research) the Gulag clearly played a significant role in the timber industry and in the production of nonferrous metals (gold, platinum, nickel, etc.). But these industries employed only a part (and a small one at that) of the "special contingents." Forced labor was of unique importance in the construction of the largest and most labor-intensive projects. This factor raises another

37. Data from S. Rosenfield, quoted in the paper by M. Van der Linden (see note 36).

38. *Naseleniye Rossii v XX veke: Istoricheskiye Ocherki.* Vol. 2, edited by Yu. A. Polyakov (Moscow, 2001), pp. 173, 181 (section author V. N. Zemskov).

39. GARF R-9414.1.326: 25, 30.

question: what was the role of these prisoner-built enterprises, railroads, canals, and so forth, in the country's actual industrialization?

We are obliged to resort to the concept of "actual industrialization" because of the commonly known fact that the Stalinist type of industrialization was extremely cost-intensive and inefficient. Huge investments were made in the construction of projects that eventually were either left unfinished or proved economically useless. The reasons this phenomenon became so widespread require separate study. But one of the reasons was obviously that the state could use large contingents of the Gulag's "cheap" and mobile labor. The accessibility of this labor encouraged economic voluntarism and made it possible to undertake expensive but economically dubious projects without particular difficulty or hesitation.

The first such project was the first significant OGPU project— the construction of the White Sea–Baltic Canal. The decision to build it resulted from a combination of two factors. First, the political one: Stalin was convinced of the military-strategic and economic importance of such a structure, and despite objections not only from the "rightist" chairman of the government, Aleksei Rykov, but also from Stalin's loyal associate, Vyacheslav Molotov, Stalin insisted on adopting the relevant plans.[40] Second, construction of the canal would probably not have been undertaken if the OGPU hadn't had a large number of prisoners because of the mass operations against the kulaks. The planned allocation of 140,000 prisoners for the BBK removed the critical problem of labor use of the camps' growing population and opened up enormous prospects for economic activities for the OGPU. Therefore the decision was mostly political, which predetermined its modest economic results.

The canal's capacity for transporting cargo for the national economy was limited. The start-up of the White Sea–Baltic Canal

40. *Pisma I. V. Stalina V. M. Molotovu. 1925–1936 gg.* Compiled by L. P. Koshelyov et al. (Moscow, 1995), pp. 214–215.

and then the Moskva-Volga Canal were of small importance, since two old connections—the Mariinsk and Moskva River systems—were not modernized.[41] In 1940 the canal was used to 44 percent of capacity, and in 1950, to 20 percent.[42] As a result, a contemporary researcher argues that the White Sea–Baltic Canal "remained as an expensive monument to the mismanagement of the Soviet system." "The canal's value to the region's economic development, as soon became clear, was minor. And strategically, the waterway's value was negligible."[43]

There are similar skeptical conclusions in the literature on another OGPU-NKVD project, the Baikal-Amur Mainline. This was one of the largest projects—at the beginning of 1938, Bamlag (BAM camp) housed more than two hundred thousand prisoners, and a few months later, it was the source for the creation of several camps. Despite the considerable material resources and labor invested in the railroad and the many casualties among prisoners, the actual results of the construction were meager. The individual sections that were put into operation were of no substantial importance. The construction of many lines was suspended.[44] "On the whole, the prewar phase of construction of the BAM, despite the large amount of work performed by three hundred thousand prisoners, ended as yet another unfinished project."[45]

The BAM (and railroad construction in general) was a typical example of how ruinous the Stalinist system of forced-labor mobilization was. The disorganized construction of many railroads with-

41. B. P. Orlov, *Razvitiye Transporta SSSR. 1917–1962* (Moscow, 1963), 198–200.

42. GARF R-5446.81b.6645: 51–53.

43. Yu. Kilin, *Kareliya v Politike Sovetskogo Gosudarstva. 1920–1941 gg.* (Petrozavodsk, 1999), pp. 122–127.

44. O. P. Yelantseva, "BAM: Pervoye Desyatiletiye," in *Otechestvennaya Istoriya*, 1994, No. 6, pp. 89–103.

45. A. G. Granberg, and V. V. Kuleshov (eds.). *Region BAM: Kontseptsiya Razvitiya na Novom Etape* (Novosibirsk, 1996), p. 9.

out the necessary feasibility studies resulted in the immobilization of enormous resources. By 1938 the length of railroads whose construction had been started but then suspended was approaching 5,000 km (excluding railroads that had been built but not used or only partly used because they weren't needed). Meanwhile, the total increase in the length of the rail system from 1933 through 1939 was only 4,500 km.[46] A substantial portion of "dead roads" were built by prisoners. Similar examples during the postwar period are well known; the most striking one is the unfinished Chum-Salekhard-Igarka railroad, whose construction in the Arctic cost the lives of many prisoners, not to mention the pointlessly expended, huge material resources valued at 3.3 billion rubles.[47]

A similar fate befell other Gulag projects. In September 1940, for example, a resolution was adopted to freeze the construction of the Kuibyshev hydroelectric system[48] started in 1937. The government attributed this decision to "a lack of free manpower" to work at an enormous new project—the construction of the Volga-Baltic and Northern Dvina water system. By the time construction was suspended, a huge sum—126.7 million rubles[49]—had already been spent on building the Kuibyshev hydroelectric system, and thirty thousand to forty thousand prisoners were concentrated at the Samara camp, which supported the project.[50] After Stalin's death, as mentioned earlier, the government was compelled to halt the construction of various enterprises and hydraulic-engineering installations, where work costing 6.3 billion rubles had already been done.[51]

46. O. P. Yelantseva, "BAM: Pervoye Desyatiletiye," p. 102.
47. GULAG (Glavnoye Upravleniye Lagerei), 1917–1960 gg., pp. 182–184.
48. RGASPI 17.3.1027: 75.
49. GARF R-5446.81b.6691: 69.
50. B. M. Smirnov, (ed.). Sistema Ispravitelno-Trudovykh Lagerei v SSSR. 1923–1960. Spravochnik (Moscow, 1998), pp. 370–371.
51. GULAG (Glavnoye Upravleniye Lagerei), 1917–1960 gg., p. 789.

This exceeded the amount of capital projects performed by the MVD in all of 1948.

So far there have been no separate studies of unfinished or useless construction by the OGPU, NKVD, and MVD. The individual examples above at least show that the camp economy's performance cannot be evaluated by the amount of nominally used capital investments. In short, here is the point. Many prisoner-built projects were difficult, or almost impossible, to build with free workers, but was there a need to build them at all? The availability of large prisoner contingents made it relatively easy to adopt plans for the accelerated construction of major projects, without making serious economic or engineering calculations, and then to scrap the projects that had been started and transfer the prisoners to new ones.

The incentive for unfinished and useless construction was only one example of the negative effect of the Gulag economy on the country's development. It is obvious, for example, that the extreme exploitation of prisoners, which might have been economically profitable for a short term, actually caused enormous damage. The untimely death of hundreds of thousands of people in the Gulag and the senseless waste of effort and talent that would have been of incomparably greater usefulness if workers had been at liberty (complaints about the use of skilled cadres for the wrong purpose—in heavy physical work—are a common topic in the institutional documents of the NKVD and MVD) substantially weakened the country's labor capability. In addition, many tens of thousands of able-bodied people who were prison guards were missing from public production.

Such endemic features of the Soviet economy as excessive bureaucratization and weak internal incentives for development reached extreme limits in the Gulag economy. The heightened secrecy and isolation promoted the proliferation at Gulag projects of padded statistics and false reports, especially since many NKVD-MVD construction projects were funded without designs and estimates but according to actual expenditures. The reminiscences of former prisoners overflow with testimony about how tenaciously and resourcefully people at the camps sought to "pull a *tufta.*" This term, which came into universal use in the Gulag, referred to the extremely wide use of padded statistics, which not only prisoners (whose lives were often saved by *tufta*) but also their bosses had a stake in preserving.

The mining industry of the NKVD and MVD was based on predatory exploitation of resources. With enormous territories and a steady flow of labor at their disposal, the heads of NKVD enterprises preferred not to set up permanent facilities that required substantial investment but sought to obtain the greatest short-term yield from the most resource-rich sites. This policy was the basis, in particular, of Dalstroi's "economic miracle" in the second half of the 1930s and of the nominal "cheapness" of Kolyma gold. But the miracle could not go on for long. Though the average gold content between 1935 and 1938 (thanks to the exploitation of the richest deposits) was 27 to 19.3 grams per cubic meter of sands washed, in 1946–47 it was already only about 7 grams. Accordingly, the amounts mined dropped sharply as well.

Despite its secrecy, the forced-labor economy couldn't function in isolation and thus had a corrupting effect on the "free" sector of the economy as well. Soviet economic ministries, which for systemic reasons didn't have much of a stake in organizational and technological progress, preferred to solve many problems by issuing "requisitions" for prisoners, which slowed down the development of the labor market and of the social infrastructure even more. Prisoner labor was becoming a narcotic for the economy.

On the whole, the transformation of the NKVD, and then the MVD, into one of the largest economic ministries and the large-scale use of forced labor in the Soviet economy between the 1930s and the 1950s were important features of the Stalinist industrialization model, in which politics, as a rule, had priority over economics. The mass political repressions and the brutal system of criminal penalties, which served as sources for expanding the forced-labor economy, were always aimed at fulfilling political objectives and in economic terms were losing operations. Only a country as rich in labor and natural resources as the Soviet Union could have weathered the physical annihilation of hundreds of thousands of able-bodied citizens, the ruin of millions of peasant farms, the maintenance of an enormous punitive apparatus, and so forth. By creating the Gulag economy, the state, above all, was attempting to lessen these enormous material losses.

In practice, however, the exploitation of prisoners ultimately increased the losses. It promoted economic voluntarism and the mindless inflation of capital-construction plans, including ruinous (and often useless) projects. When more detailed studies are done, they will most likely show that the role of forced labor in building up *actual* industrial capability was far smaller than the formal economic indicators of the NKVD and MVD show.

The End of the Gulag

Aleksei Tikhonov

STALIN DIED ON March 5, 1953. The principal portfolios were distributed immediately—Lavrenty Beria nominated Georgy Malenkov for chairman of the Council of Ministers, and Malenkov proposed Beria as his first deputy while naming him as minister of the newly consolidated Ministry of Internal Affairs and State Security (MVD). In the course of the following week, Beria issued directives that closed all of the highly publicized political cases under way, such as the "Kremlin doctors' plot" and the "Mengrelian affair." On March 26 he sent the Presidium of the Central Committee a proposed decree "On amnesty."[1] This decree called for the release of about one million inmates from Gulag camps, colonies, and prisons and cut in half the terms of those left in camps. The next day (!) the amnesty decree was published in the central press, and over the next three months some 1.5 million prisoners, or about 60 percent of the entire Gulag population, were released. This virtual dismantling of the Gulag camp system was carried out in such a short time, considering the vast geographic

1. L. Beria, 1953. Documents, Moscow 1999. Published as a joint project of the Democracy International Foundation and the Hoover Institution.

scope of the Gulag empire, that it became the basis of a conspiracy theory advanced by Khrushchev as the justification for Beria's execution. According to Khrushchev, Beria deliberately released a large number of criminals to strengthen the MVD to make himself the new dictator. Beria was so compromised by these accusations that the rather absurd myth of the "conspiratorial" motives for the amnesty became part of history courses taught in Russian schools. Beria's control of the secret police would have given him a more direct method of dealing with his rivals.

The scale of the 1953 amnesty made it not so much a political measure as a social and economic one. Like a military demobilization, the amnesty required a strategy and a plan. The three weeks that elapsed between Stalin's death and the amnesty announcement were clearly insufficient to prepare a plan for the large-scale amnesty of 1.5 million prisoners. Presumably, such a plan was waiting in the wings pending Stalin's death. Indeed, the Gulag archives reveal earlier planning within the Gulag system for radical restructuring.[2] As far back as 1930, the eventual architect of the Gulag system, G. Yagoda, proposed exile with accompanying family members as a superior alternative to camps. The MVD administration had been trying since the late 1940s to "cleanse" the camps of most of their inmates. Two actual MVD plans (from 1949 and 1951) called for the conversion of Gulag prisoners into an exile labor force. Both plans were associated with S. S. Mamulov—deputy minister of internal affairs from 1946 to 1953—an official from Beria's inner circle who was repressed in 1953 along with Beria. Moral issues were not a motive for the proposed changes; the MVD's main concern was to strengthen the camp regime for the remaining inmates while meeting its production goals. Notably, the two MVD plans did not call for an amnesty, which would have had to originate with the Politburo. Rather they proposed to send camp inmates into exile

2. These files are located in the Hoover Institution Archives, Fond 9414.

in remote regions, on the mandatory condition that they work at the MVD industrial and construction projects.

The first plan was proposed in an internal MVD document from 1949. The deputy minister of internal affairs, V. V. Chernyshev (who headed the Gulag from 1939 to 1941), sent Mamulov a proposal to transfer all inmates in the camps of the Pechora Territory of northern Russia after five years' confinement to the status of special resettlers, assigned to the Pechora Coal Basin for their ten- to twenty-year sentences.[3] Chernyshev enclosed a Draft Resolution for the Council of Ministers, signed by the Gulag's chief, G. P. Dobrynin, which demonstrates its serious intent.[4] Besides release from the camps, the plan required the MVD "to provide opportunities for exiled settlers to set up personal households and to render assistance in the construction of individual houses."[5] Settlers had the right to summon their families to their places of exile. Unfortunately, no traces of the debate over this plan survive in the archives, although events show that it was not implemented. In fact, the Chernyshev proposal was typical of the Soviet approach to major reforms. The reform was to be tried out first on a limited experimental basis before its coverage was expanded. In this instance, the new system applied to only one camp region, but in 1949, even this modest reform proposal went too far.

Again in June of 1951, Mamulov sent to MVD minister S. N. Kruglov a bold initiative for reorganizing the Gulag. Mamulov's letter did not survive, but the Gulag archives contain abundant material on the subsequent debate inside the MVD, which makes Mamulov's own proposals clear. The Mamulov proposal is summarized in a memo prepared by a Colonel Liamin, the head of the MVD's organization department, on June 18, 1951, as Agenda

3. 9414-1d-146, l. 3.
4. 9414-1d-146, ll. 7–8.
5. 9414-1d-146, l. 8.

Point 14: "About the replacement of the term of confinement by exile to remote regions of persons convicted of certain crimes." This agenda item was rejected in a June 19 meeting of the administration of the MVD, for the reasons spelled out in a memo to Kruglov, written by the director of the Gulag administration, I. Dolgikh, on July 6.[6]

As in the 1949 proposal, the 1951 Mamulov proposal called for the replacement of camp sentences with exile to remote areas for persons convicted of specified crimes. Though the 1949 proposal had been limited to one camp region, the 1951 Mamulov proposal called for the transfer of almost 70 percent of all inmates in camps and colonies to the status of exiles, which meant a reorganization of the entire Gulag system. Only the most hardened criminals would remain in camps. The advantages of the reorganization were that the state would be relieved of its obligations to pay 8 billion rubles a year from the state budget for the support of prisoners; the use of convict labor would improve; and the regime for guarding the especially dangerous offenders remaining in camps would be improved, reducing the incidence of escapes. The provisions of Soviet labor law would apply to exiles, although wages would be lower. In other words, the new "exiles" would have a juridical status halfway between Gulag inmates and free workers.

The discussion summarized in the July 6 memo to the minister of the MVD shows that it was not possible to adopt such a sweeping proposal in 1951. The Gulag chief, Dolgikh, objected that implementation of this plan "would require a radical reorganization of the work of enterprises and construction projects at which manpower from the camps is used, causing serious damage to the country's economy." Moreover, a change in the status of almost 75 percent of prisoners (1,790,000) would mean revising the entire penal code, which had focused after the war on the prosecution of

6. 9414-1-504, ll. 2–5.

crimes against state and personal property. Under Mamulov's proposal, prisoners converted to exile status would be largely those who had stolen state or private property; prisoners remaining in camps would be largely those convicted of violent crimes. Moreover, Dolgikh objected that many repeat offenders would be set free and that the new system would require extensive capital expenditures. Because of such objections, Mamulov's proposal was rejected, although the Gulag did acknowledge the need "to develop a practice of paroling inmates and transferring them to exile status." In fact, the MVD administration welcomed the principle of selective conversion of Gulag prisoners to exiles if they had earned the right through hard work and good behavior. Particularly objectionable was Mamulov's proposal to convert to exile status all prisoners sentenced under specific criminal codes regardless of their work or behavior. Rewarding of prisoners by converting them to exiles should be used as an incentive.

The handling of the Mamulov proposal was typical of the Soviet bureaucracy. The proposal was made by a deputy; the proposal was then discussed by the collegium of the ministry (the MVD), and a decision was reached and sent to the minister. Even though the proposed change was substantial, the proposal did not constitute a political initiative. Rather, it involved an internal discussion of the classification of sentenced persons under the jurisdiction of the MVD, either as Gulag inmates or as exiles, although, as the discussion shows, there was concern that such a move would change the existing criminal codex. The discussion shows the MVD trying to find better methods for holding "dangerous" prisoners while meeting its production goals. The Mamulov proposal was not a theoretical exercise. It provided a list of 1.8 million Gulag inmates for conversion to exile status according to the criminal code under which they had been sentenced.

Mamulov's list remained within the MVD for another two years. The death of Stalin in March of 1953 provided the oppor-

Table 4.1   Comparison of Mamulov's 1951 "Exile" Proposal with Beria's 1953 Amnesty

Laws and Decrees	1951 Mamulov	1953 Amnesty
Theft of socialist property (August 7, 1932, law)	4%	4%
Theft of personal property (Article 47)	24%	24%
Theft of public property (Article 47)	35%	33%
Profiteering	4%	5%
Property crimes	4%	3%
Hooliganism	5%	7%
Violation of the law on the internal passport system	2%	2%
Crimes by soldiers	2%	3%
Official and economic crimes	7%	8%
Decrees other than those listed above	2%	2%
Other crimes	8%	7%
Totals (millions)	1.8	1.5

tunity for the new leadership, at first under Malenkov and Beria, to make the political decision to dismantle the Gulag system. The amnesty decree initially freed more than 1.5 million prisoners, while the Mamulov proposal called for the exile of 1.8 million prisoners to remote regions for work on MVD projects. Table 4.1 shows that the 1953 amnesty actually followed Mamulov's plan. The percentages of those granted amnesty in 1953 (according to the crime that they had committed) were nearly identical to those proposed in 1951 for transfer to exile status.

The stereotype of the Soviet system is that government agencies were mainly interested in protecting their turf and in building their own empires. According to this stereotype, the MVD and the Gulag administration should have wanted as large a Gulag system as possible. In reality, a consistent theme throughout the Gulag archives is that the Gulag system cost more than it produced and that it was creating a class of professional criminals. Internal Gulag studies showed extraordinarily high rates of recidivism with those initially sentenced for minor crimes, especially young people, returning as repeat offenders charged with more serious crimes. Although there were some apparent successes in the use of prison labor for large construction projects in the early 1930s, the Gulag became a drain on the economy and the state budget as it filled with victims of the Great Terror and then with returning Soviet POWs. The 1953 amnesty derived primarily from the bureaucratic interests of the MVD itself. An external event—Stalin's death—merely provided an excuse for the radical reform, which had been desired by the MVD and Gulag administration itself for many years. The amnesty on the occasion of Stalin's death protected the MVD leadership against charges of attempting to change Soviet criminal law.

The irony of this "beginning of the end" of the Gulag system is that the real author of the amnesty, Mamulov, later served fifteen years in prison himself and was not covered by the amnesty. Beria, the feared MVD minister, suffered an even worse fate: he was the last major political figure in Soviet history to be executed.

Coercion versus Motivation
Forced Labor in Norilsk

Leonid Borodkin and Simon Ertz

CHAPTER 7 COVERS the history of Noril-lag, the correctional labor camp founded to provide penal labor for the vast mineral wealth of Norilsk. That chapter focuses on the construction of a large-scale industrial complex, a task imposed on the NKVD's Gulag administration in 1935. Although labor issues are addressed parenthetically, Chapter 7 deals mainly with the relationship between Norilsk and its NKVD and Politburo superiors. The current chapter turns to the subject of forced labor—how Noril-lag organized and motivated prison workers to complete the planned tasks for which Norilsk's bosses were held accountable.

Norillag was one of the largest Gulag facilities, employing close to one hundred thousand workers at its peak. It was one of the Gulag's highest-priority camps, producing metals vital to the Soviet industry and military. Norilsk's priority status was shown by its direct subordination to the director of the Gulag from its founding in 1935 until 1941. The Norilsk Integrated Plant played a central role in the country's nickel industry in the 1940s. When transferred from the MVD to civilian industry in 1954, Norilsk was producing one-quarter of Soviet nickel.

Chapters 1 and 3 emphasized the perceived advantages of forced labor that could be seized upon by a dictator like Stalin: Unlike free workers who demanded substantial material incentives to work in remote regions, prisoners could be dispatched by administrative decree. Their labor could be closely monitored by guards; their hours of work could be set by administrative order, and poor work punished. The use of punishment rather than material rewards saved vital resources, and "surpluses" could be extracted from prison workers. Chapter 2 shows that Soviet labor policy mixed "carrots and sticks" even in the periods of greatest coercion in the work place. This chapter finds that even in the Gulag, where force could be most conveniently applied, camp administrators combined material incentives with overt coercion.

In a penal labor environment, camp administrators could induce inmates to fulfill their "plans" by four general methods: rules, punishments, moral incentives, and material incentives. Rules set forth the planned tasks of prisoners, such as the number of work hours or piece-rate norms. By stiffening rules and regulations to make inmates work harder and longer, more "surplus" could be extracted. Punishments, such as reduced rations or solitary confinement, maintained discipline; moral incentives, such as medals or other honors, encouraged the fulfillment of tasks without a loss of scarce resources; and material incentives, such as higher pay, differentially rewarded those with the best work records.

NORILSK'S PRIORITY

Figure 5.1 shows Norillag's labor force compared with total Gulag labor.[1] The number of Norilsk prisoners grew rapidly and steadily

---

1. More precisely, we have statistical data from the Gulag's Records and Assignments Department, which produced regular reports on prisoners at all camps, including Norilsk, and reports from Norilsk itself on contingents of prisoners and free employees. Norilsk reports cover 1936–38 and 1941–49. GARF 9414 (Gulag); 8361 (GULGMP).

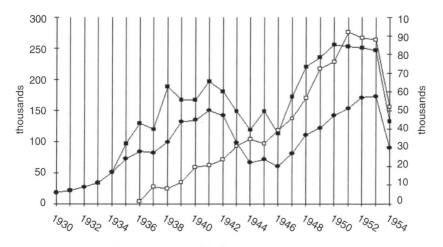

-■- Number of prisoners in all camps and colonies of NKVD/MVD
-●- Number of prisoners in camps of NKVD/MVD
-□- Number of prisoners in Norillag and Gorny camp

Figure 5.1   A Comparison of the Number of Prisoners in Norillag and Gorny Camps with the Number of Prisoners at All Camps and Colonies of the NKVD-MVD (January 1 of Each Year)
Sources: For Norilsk—GARF 9414.1.174: 7; 1155: 20, 54ob., 55; 1160: 4; 2784: 18; 1.358: 1, 17, 29, 55; 364: 2, 19, 37, 54; 370: 24, 60; 371: 2, 29, 54, 70; 379: 15, 92ob.; 390: 2, 47, 85, 129; 424: 8, 58, 114, 165; 442: 1, 45, 88, 130; 455: 8; 466: 10, 57ob., 103ob., 146ob.; 472: 2ob., 17ob., 18ob., 42ob., 64ob.; 479: 3ob., 27ob., 51ob., 75ob.; 485: 3ob., 21ob., 25ob., 40ob., 58ob., 78; 495: 2ob., 21ob., 39ob., 57ob.; 500: 2ob., 31ob., 46ob., 58ob.; 502: 1, 4, 7, 10; 506: 15ob., 47ob., 48ob., 73ob., 74ob., 110ob.; 508: 4; 511: 8ob., 67ob., 124ob., 150ob.; 513: 3ob., 39ob., 70ob. For other camps and colonies: GARF 9414. 1. 1155: 1a, 2. For 1949–1954 data, see: Zemskov, V. N. "GULAG (istoriko-sotsiologichesky aspekt)," in *Sotsiologicheskiye Issledovaniya,* No. 6, 1991, p. 11; No. 7, 1991, p. 12. Camp data for 1954 are as of April 1.

until the end of 1950. There were only two years of decline, 1937 and 1944. Norillag peaked at the beginning of 1951, when it housed ninety-two thousand prisoners in twenty-four camp divisions, twenty-three separate and regular camp centers, and six other units, including its mining camp.[2] National prisoner totals, on the other

2. Data for October 1, 1951. GARF 9414.1.461: 53.

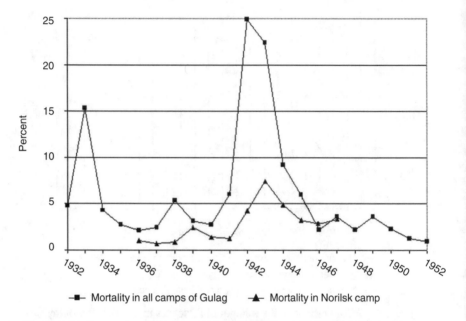

Figure 5.2   Comparison of Prisoner Mortality Rates at All NKVD Camps with Those at Norilsk (Morbidity as a Percentage of Average Annual Population)
Sources: GARF 9414.1.2740: 34, 43, 49, 62, 85; 2784: 7-10, 26; 2788: 3, 6, 9, 11, 15, 17, 19, 24, 27, 30, 33, 34; 2796: 97, 102ob.-103, 114ob., 128, 141, 247; 2804: 2ob.-3, 39; 2817: 2, 11, 21, 30, 39, 48; 2821: 31ob., 118ob.; 2822: 61ob.-62, 126ob.-127; 2883: 114, 116.

hand, rose with the mass repressions in the late 1930s, the toughening of penitentiary policy in mid-1947, and the appearance of new classes of prisoners with World War II. In the absence of new repressions, the camp population declined because of mortality, the dispatch of prisoners to the front during World War II, and amnesties, such as those of 1945 and 1953. Norillag, in contrast, grew steadily and independently of the growth of the camp system as a whole, reflecting the high priority of its economic tasks and its importance as a supplier of priority metals to the economy and military.

Mortality in Norillag should have been naturally high because of its location in the Arctic Circle, but Figure 5.2 shows that its mortality rate was considerably lower than Gulag averages,[3] even during the war when meager food supplies and poor medical care raised general Gulag mortality. In 1942 and 1943 the average mortality rate at all camps was 25 percent—one-fourth of the entire camp population died in a year!—while the corresponding Norilsk figure averaged 5.5 percent. Norilsk's low mortality rate indicates that prisoners were in relatively good physical condition. The managers of Gulag camps had a stake in keeping prisoners healthy so that their plans could be met. In fact, prisoners' work was regulated according to the state of their health, as a lecture for internal use by the director of the Gulag, V. G. Nasedkin, relates: "Physically healthy prisoners are assigned to Work Capacity Category 1, which allows them to be used for heavy physical work. Prisoners with minor physical deficiencies (non-organic functional disorders) are placed in Work Capacity Category 2 and are used in medium-heavy work. Prisoners with pronounced physical deficiencies and diseases are assigned Work Capacity Category 3 and are used in light physical work and individual physical work. Prisoners with severe physical deficiencies that preclude their use for labor are assigned to Category 4—the disabled category. Hence all of the labor processes that pertain to the production structure of each camp are divided, according to how arduous the work is, into heavy, medium and light. . . ."[4] Norilsk had the extra advantage that medical examinations and the selection of prisoners for Norilsk were done at the sites from which prisoners were dispatched. Prisoners deemed unable to work in the Arctic were not sent to Norilsk, as several

---

3. The source of these data is the statistics of prisoner morbidity and mortality, which the Gulag's health department gathered to monitor the prisoners' physical condition, devise measures to improve it, and to lower the mortality rate.

4. GARF 9414.1.77: 26-27. The document is dated 1945 or 1946, but in any case no later than February 21, 1947.

former prisoners have testified.[5] The percentage of prisoners capable only of light physical work (or less) dispatched to Norilsk was small, particularly since such prisoners accounted for one-third of the Gulag population in 1942.[6] The selection of relatively healthy prisoners, however, was not the only reason for Norilsk's low mortality rate. Personal testimonies of former Norillag prisoners confirm that, although living conditions at Norillag were harsh and food sources meager, these conditions were still somewhat better than at other labor camps.

Camps in the Gulag used a standard system, introduced in 1935, for prisoner record keeping.[7] Prisoners were divided into Group A prisoners, who worked in production or construction; Group B prisoners, who occupied administrative-managerial and support jobs; Group C and D prisoners, who were not working because of illness, transit, quarantine, solitary confinement, or work refusal. Camp administrators aimed to limit Group C and D workers and raise the proportion of actively working prisoners. In Norilsk, Group A workers constituted more than 80 percent of all prisoners as compared with the Gulag average of 70 to 75 percent in the 1940s, while the share of nonworking prisoners did not exceed 10 percent.

Another indicator of Norilsk's priority status was its widespread use of free workers. In 1941, a total of 3,734 free workers and 16,532 prisoners worked at the Norilsk plant, or a ratio of approximately 1:5; by 1949 this ratio had decreased to 1:2.1 (20,930 free

5. See, for example S. S. Torvin, "Vospominaniya" in the Archives of the Moscow Memorial Scholarly Information and Educational Center (hereafter Moscow Memorial Archives), 2.2.92: l. 90; N. Semakin (reminiscences; untitled). Ibid., 2.3.58; I. Assanov, "Zhizn' i Sudba Mitrofana Petrovicha Rubeko," in *Norilsky Memorial*, No. 4, October 1998, p. 11.

6. GARF 9414.1.370: 90.

7. Directive No. 664871 of the director of the Gulag, March 11, 1935. See A. I. Kokurin, N. V. Petrov, and Yu. Morukov. "GULAG: Struktura i Kadry" in *Svobodnaya Mysl'*, 1999, No. 9, pp. 116–117.

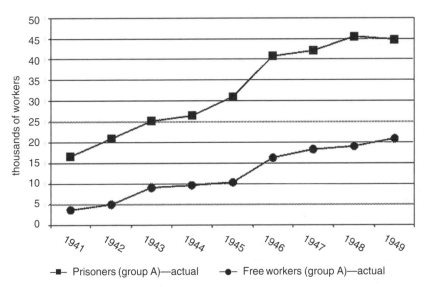

Figure 5.3   The Integrated Plant's Labor Resources—Number of Free Workers and Group A Prisoners (Production Workers) (Average Annual Totals)
Sources: GARF 8361.1.10: 11; 11: 11, 27, 32; 40: 26; 56: 44-45; 71: 30; 95: 109; 101: 124-125; 125: 158; 143: 54; 155: 145; 174: 102.

workers and 44,897 prisoners), as shown in Figure 5.3. In 1936 free workers numbered 223 compared with 4,552 prisoners in all sectors (including workers in all groups), and in 1937, free workers numbered 384 compared with 8,658 prisoners.[8] The increase in free workers during subsequent years in Norilsk resulted mostly from the release of prisoners—a process that followed different paths. During the 1940s prisoners were commonly assigned to the plant even after they had nominally completed their sentences. Many released prisoners, especially political ones, were sent to a "special settlement" as exiles with internal passports that often barred them even from leaving the city limits of Norilsk. There were instances, for example, where a prisoner, shortly before his term ended, was

8. GARF 9414.1.854: 78, 81; 969: 59–62.

informed, virtually without explanation, of a "second term."[9] Such measures are explained by Norilsk's persistent need for labor, especially during the war, when nickel production had to be increased as rapidly as possible. The plant's free workers were covered by a certificate that exempted them from being drafted into the Red Army,[10] and prisoners' requests for transfer to the front were generally denied.[11] The Norilsk administration saw to it that even prisoners who, under the Supreme Soviet resolution, were to be released early for the front, continued to work as prisoners.[12] A State Defense Committee decision issued on January 19, 1945, shortly before the end of the war, released workers from custody and then attached them to the Norilsk plant as free workers.[13] In the first half of 1946, more than twelve thousand former prisoners were assigned to Norilsk under a special resolution of the State Defense Committee. Beginning in the second half of 1946, they were gradually converted to the status of ordinary free workers.[14] It remains unclear, however, whether they received full rights, including the right to leave Norilsk.

The economic and juridical position of the two classes of free workers—former prisoners and those who had come to Norilsk without previously serving in the camp—was substantially different. Unlike newcomers, former Norilsk prisoners were deprived of benefits and privileges for work in the Far North. In the second half

9. N. V. Numerov, *Zolotaia Zvezda GULAGa* (Moscow: Izd-vo zhurn, 1999), pp. 402–403.

10. Ye. Kersnovskaya, *Skol'ko Stoit Chelovek* (Moscow: Fond Kersnvskoi, 2001), vol. 4, p. 220.

11. P. O. Sagoyan, *Vospominania* (untitled), in Moscow Memorial Archives, 2.1.104: 23; I. Assanov, *Zhizn' i Sud'ba Mitrofana Petrovicha Rubeko*, "Noril'skiy Memorial," edition 4, October, 1998, place of publication not given, p. 12.

12. GARF 9414.1.1188: 11ob. See also Zemskov, Ukaz. soch., *Sotsiologicheskie Issledovania*, No. 7, 1991, p. 24.

13. GARF 9414.1.1188, pp. 11, 13, 24, 37-39.

14. GARF 9414.1.447:1ob., 2, 14ob., 15, 22ob., 23, 38ob., 39; 457: 2ob., 3.

of the 1940s, free workers who entered into Norilsk labor contracts for three years received a 100 percent "northern increment" and an extra 10 percent for each month. After two and a half years, they were given a six-month paid vacation, free transportation, and a month for traveling back and forth. Those who signed on for another three years got the same terms and a voucher to a sanatorium for the entire length of the vacation."[15] In 1945 a "special contingent" of more than ten thousand former Soviet prisoners of war and Vlasovites was settled in Norilsk on the same basis as exiles—they received northern benefits, but they were not allowed to leave Norilsk. After screening by the camp's Special Department, many of these "special contingents" were sentenced to terms of confinement, mostly under Art. 58-1b (treason by a serviceman).[16]

Most "free" workers in Norilsk had a camp background, were restricted in their movements, and did not receive special wage supplements. "Released hard workers" deprived of such benefits formed a stratum of "second-class people" in the late 1940s.[17] Norilsk management used these restrictions to lower labor costs even after prisoners were released. A 1950 report by the director of Norillag, V. S. Zverev, revealed that only 20 percent of free workers were actually "free": "The 25,000 free workers at the plant's production facilities include 15,000 ex-convicts, 3,997 special settlers and 1,000 exiles. . . ."[18]

15. E. Setko-Setkevich, "Bozhe, Spasi Dushu Moiu," *Vospominania Sibiriakov* (Warsaw, 1990), p. 9, cited from "Noril'skiy Memorial," edition 3, October 1996, place of publication not given (translation of B. S. Birger).

16. S. S. Torvin, "Vospominania," Arkhiv Moskovskogo Nauchno-Informatsionnogo I Prosvetotel'skogo Tsentra "Memorial," l. 131. The author dates the appearance of the "special contingent" to August 1946, in which he is apparently mistaken, since the archives say that these people were first taken to Norilsk in August 1945. See GARF 9414.1.430: 26ob., 27, 30, 33ob., 34; 447: 1ob., 2, 14ob., 15, 22ob., 23, 38ob., 39.

17. S. S. Torvin, "Vospominania" (f.2. op.2. d.92. l.129).

18. GARF 9414.1.151: 33.

Although penal and free labor worked together in production and construction, free labor was used primarily in production. The most labor-intensive and grueling jobs, mainly in construction, were for prisoners; other jobs could be performed by both free workers and prisoners. Prisoners represented an all-purpose labor resource for the Norilsk plant.

Although accounts from other camps suggest that prisoners were not used according to their specialty, former Norilsk inmates report that prisoners were used in their profession at the proper levels. The rational use of specialists was often attributed to A. Zavenyagin, the second director of the integrated plant (which was later named for him) from April 1938 through March 1941. But the use of prisoners according to specialization was actually general Gulag policy, as shown by a 1940 order by Interior Minister L. Beria: ". . . I order . . . that full use be made of all specialists among prisoners [only 623 out of 1,200 specialists at the Norilsk plant are being used in their specialty], primarily in production, and the most qualified of them as technical supervisors."[19] Hence the use of qualified specialist-prisoners in responsible positions in Norilsk was not an isolated initiative by Zavenyagin but a general policy of the Gulag and the NKVD. Prisoners working in their specialty could not be sure their assignment would be permanent. When the war broke out, the Norilsk camp management removed prisoners from management positions, either for security reasons or to make positions for party functionaries avoiding call-ups to the front.[20] Starting in 1943, when the Red Army's prospects on the front improved markedly, prisoners (even political ones) again were given the chance to work in their specialties. Nevertheless, in Norillag, from 90 to 95

19. NKVD Order No. 0424 of September 27, 1940, "On Measures to Improve the Work of the Norilsk Integrated Plant."
20. Kersnovskaya, *op. cit.*, p. 220.

percent of all prisoners were employed as ordinary workers. Opportunities to have skilled jobs, specifically as engineers or technicians, were granted only to a small group of prisoners. Such positions were not only physically less taxing, but they offered better rations and benefits.[21] Engineering and technical jobs were reserved mainly for "free" labor. In construction, 3 to 5 percent of prisoners, compared with 30 percent of free workers, had engineering and technical positions. In 1944 there were far more free workers than prisoners in specialized construction positions.

REGULATING WORK EFFORT

Work "effort" is determined by quantity, measured by hours worked per unit of time, and by quality, measured by the worker's effectiveness. The quantity of work is easier to regulate than its quality. Unsurprisingly, Norilsk inmates worked long hours with few days off. According to a lecture designated for internal use, Gulag inmates in the 1940s were granted four days off a month.[22] General instructions for Gulag camps from the spring of 1947 granted eight special days off (January 22, May 1 and 2, May 9, September 3, November 7–8 and December 5). According to Norillag statistics, after 1945 the annual number of workdays declined to about 300 to 310 and then stabilized at this level. Norillag's figures are consistent with general Gulag regulations which granted four days off a month and eight additional days off a year, yielding 309 workdays. Prisoners under a hard-labor regime in the mid-1940s had only three days off a month,[23] a figure which was raised to four days in July 1950.

21. F. I. Vintens, "Vospominania," without title, Moskovskiy Arkhiv "Memorial" (f.2. op.2 d.11. l.33).
22. GARF 9414.1.77: 28.
23. Ibid., 56.

Figure 5.4   Average Number of Days Worked by Group A Prisoners per Year in Norilsk

	1941	1942	1943	1944*	1945	1946	1947	1948*	1949
Plan	293	317	313	300	329	317	312	302	308
Actual	335	349	329	328	320	309	296	307	308

Note: *1944 and 1948 were leap years.
Source: GARF 8361.1.11: 31; 40; 41; 56; 39; 71; 55; 95; 99; 101; 155; 125; 152; 155; 139; 174; 97.

We do not have the Gulag regulations for the entire period, but we do have Norillag records on the labor use of prisoners. Norillag administrators calculated how the camp's total "man-days" (the average number of all prisoners multiplied by the number of days in the given year) were spent at work and away from work, including time off. From these figures, Figure 5.4 shows the average number of days worked a year by Group A (industrial and construction) workers, a number that confirms the heavy workload of prisoners. The high point of hours worked was reached in 1942 when prisoners averaged only one and a half days off each month. As the 1942 annual report on capital investments by the Norilsk Integrated Plant stated: "A cutback in days off was a resource that made up for the manpower shortage, both in the mass vocations and in the skilled professions, and explains why the number of man-days worked was 126.5 percent of the plan while the number of workers in 1942 was 105 percent of the plan."[24] Former prisoners confirmed the extremely large number of days worked a year, although strangely enough, they provided scanty information, probably assuming that such information was common knowledge. Z. A. Ravdel, a Norillag prisoner beginning in 1939, wrote that there were no days off or holidays at all at the beginning of the war, and only after the victory

24. GARF 8361.1.41: 21ob.

at Stalingrad were two days off a month granted.[25] N. F. Odolinskaya, who was sent to Norillag under a hard-labor regime in 1945, wrote that she did not have days off even after the war.[26] After transfer to the women's hard-labor zone of the Mining Camp in the spring of 1949,[27] she wrote that "hard-labor prisoners were not allowed to celebrate Soviet holidays.[28] The first days off for hard-labor prisoners came in the early 1950s.[29] N. V. Numerov, who worked in the Mining Camp office in the spring of 1953, wrote that there were no days off for prisoners who worked there as specialists.[30] Another prisoner, M. P. Rubeko, who arrived in Norilsk in 1939, said that before the war "every Sunday was considered a day off. True, if there was urgent work, it could be canceled."[31]

Norillag had a special system for canceling work in extreme weather. During the early years of camp construction, extreme weather was handled informally, by shortening the workday or by providing breaks for warming up.[32] In 1939, General Director Zavenyagin issued an order ". . . that restricted work outside at temperatures below −40° [C] or when winds exceeded 22 m per second."[33] According to former prisoners, if the sum of temperature and wind speed reached −40°C/−42°C, then the weather was "certified" as unfit for work, and prisoners were brought back to the camp or

25. Z. I. Ravdel, "Vospominania," without title, Moskovskiy Arkhiv "Memorial" (f.2. op.1 d.100. l.157, 162–163).

26. N. F. Odolinskaya, "Sovietskiye Katorzhniki" (reminiscences), in Moscow Memorial Archives, 2.2.66: 31.

27. Odolinskaya, *op. cit.*: 80, 87.

28. Ibid., 91.

29. Ibid., 133-134.

30. Numerov, *op. cit.*, p. 402.

31. Assanov, *op. cit.*, p. 12.

32. GARF 9414.1.854: 20.

33. V. N. Lebedinsky, "V Serdtse Rudnogo Pritaimyrya" in *Voprosy Istorii*, No. 1, 1978, pp. 204–209, here p. 208.

were not taken to work at all.[34] These rules did not apply to those who worked inside buildings or in mines. During snowstorms they walked to work along ropes that had been stretched between poles.[35] For hard-labor prisoners at the Mining Camp ". . . certified weather was revoked. They were taken to work in any weather. . . ."[36] Norilsk's own statistics reveal that harsh weather rules were often disregarded. "Idle time due to atmospheric conditions" averaged only 1.55 days in 1946, 2 days in 1947, and 6 days in 1949 for the entire worker population.[37] Since certified weather applied only to outside work, the number of days of idle time would have been higher for outside workers than these figures show. According to meteorological data, the "severe weather formula" applied to at least 33 days between October and May, far more than the days actually granted.

In the mid-1940s, the Gulag administration set "the length of the workday at nine hours for prisoners engaged in unhealthy production and underground work, and at ten hours for all other work, including one hour for a lunch break."[38] In 1947, the Gulag set a nine-hour workday (also including a one-hour lunch break). Prisoners in strict-regime camps had a ten-hour workday by an order of the MVD of December 1948.[39] Hard-labor prisoners worked one hour longer than other prisoners did.[40] Former Norilsk prisoners report that they actually worked a ten-hour day, not including lunch breaks, prisoner assembly, or the time needed for getting back and forth to work. Former prisoner Z. I. Ravdel describes round-the-

34. Cheburekin, P. V. Vospominania in Moscow Memorial Archives, 2.1.125: 15–16. Vintens, *op. cit.*, l. 32; Odolinskaya, *op. cit.*, l. 33.

35. Ravdel, *op. cit.*, l. 114.

36. Odolinskaya, *op. cit.*, l. 91.

37. GARF 8361.1.56: 39; 71: 55; 95: 99; 101: 155; 125: 152; 155: 139; 174: 97.

38. GARF 9414.1.77: 28.

39. [MVD Order No. 001516 of December 31, 1948—not yet declassified.]

40. GARF 9414.1.77: 55. See also GARF 9414.1.729: 8.

clock tunneling work, which proceeded ". . . in two shifts of eleven hours each," both in 1940 and during the war.[41] Yevgeniya Kurbatova reported that in 1944 women engaged in ore sorting on a round-the-clock, two-shift schedule, worked twelve hours without breaks. Another female prisoner, E. Kersonovskaia, was supposed to work an eight-hour day doing heavy lifting. But she reported for 1944: "They don't look at the clock; they look at cars to be loaded."[42] In the 1940s another former female prisoner, who worked under a strict security regime building the Norilsk airport, reported an "official" twelve-hour day, not including going to and from work.[43]

PUNISHMENTS AND INCENTIVES

It would appear that camps offered an ideal environment for mechanisms to stimulate work effort. The work of prisoners could be monitored and poor work punished. Indeed, Gulag labor was regulated by harsh measures. The "Temporary instructions concerning the regime for holding prisoners in corrective-labor camps and colonies" issued by the NKVD on August 2, 1939, placed prisoners refusing work on a "penalty regime," and hardcore "work refusers" were subject to criminal punishments. Depending upon the violation of work discipline, workers could be deprived of correspondence for six months, deprived of the use of their own money for three months, transferred to general work (for specialists and office personnel), placed in isolation for twenty days, or placed on reduced rations and in poorer living conditions. The administration of every

41. Ravdel, *op. cit.:* 118, 157.
42. Kersnovskaia, *op. cit.,* l. 17, 26.
43. Odolinskaia, *op. cit.,* l. 29–30.

camp fought a constant battle against *tufta*, a hidden form of work refusal, or the imitation of work.[44]

In camps, as in the economy as a whole, labor-motivation systems were directed at the fulfillment of work norms. It is important to note that Gulag work norms were the same as civilian norms; norms were dictated according to the branch of the economy. Norilsk used the same work norms as its corresponding civilian branches despite its location in the Arctic Circle (see Chapter 7). Some decrees lowered norms for "physically weak" workers.[45] As might be expected, prisoner living standards depended on the fulfillment of norms. Norm underfulfillment typically meant reduced rations,[46] but the method of lowering rations had to be used cautiously. Reduced rations could so weaken workers that they could not fulfill their norms, and even severer long-term consequences, such as dysentery and tuberculosis, were often observed in Norilsk.[47] On the flip side, prisoners who overfulfilled their norms received better rations and other advantages. Such penalties and rewards were often applied to the work brigade; thus the work of one prisoner affected the rations and living conditions of other brigade members. Within the brigade, there were mechanisms for maintaining work discipline and for helping other (weaker) brigade members, such as material incentives and punishments and

44. It is not surprising that there are few sources about this phenomenon. For Norilsk see, for example, GARF 9414.1.854: 12; see also N. Suprunenko, "Ne Iskazhaia Istoriu," Norilskiy Memorial. First edition. April 1990, pp. 4–7. (This text was written in 1977 for the newspaper *Krasnoiarskiy Komsomolets,* p. 7, but was not published.)

45. GARF 8361.1.69: 22.

46. Since the problem of food and provisions in camps should be analyzed separately, Order No. 00943 NKVD of August 14, 1939, is only mentioned here. By this decree, detailed programs of the food and clothing norms for prisoners of camps and colonies were established, including schemes for the increase and decrease of norms.

47. Kersnovskaia, *op. cit.,* l. 237.

awards.[48] Brigade leaders were chosen "from the most disciplined and conscientious workers" and were responsible for fulfillment of norms.[49] The brigade leaders who achieved good work results received better rations, honorary posting on the "red board," better clothing, and the right to buy goods in the company store.[50] Prisoners could also receive commendations that were placed in the prisoner's record, monetary rewards, rewards in kind, the right to receive packages without restrictions, the right to send money to relatives not exceeding one hundred rubles a month, and the opportunity to transfer to more qualified work. Prisoners working according to "Stakhanovite" measures received added privileges, such as a place in better living quarters, boots or coats, special rations, a separate dining room or the right to be served first, first access to books or newspapers in the prison library, the best seating in the camp theater, or a place in a training course to raise qualifications.[51] In 1943, about 18 percent of prisoners and 32 percent of "free" workers were Stakhanovites.[52]

Incentives, which directly linked inmate living conditions to labor productivity, were powerful motivators for prisoners living at the margin of subsistence. They raised the productivity of successful workers and required only small managerial expenditures on bonuses. On the other hand, the loss of manpower caused by deprivation and severe working and living conditions raised serious questions about the economic effectiveness of this incentive system.

48. For a description of this process, see Ravdel', *op. cit.*, l. 154. Odolinskaia, *op. cit.*, l. 104.
49. See also Ravdel', *op. cit.*, l. 110.
50. Ravdel', *op. cit.*, l. 120.
51. Order No. 00889 NKVD of August 2, 1939.
52. GARF 8361.1.57: 22–23, 38b.

WORK CREDITS FOR REDUCED TERMS

The Gulag administration used a "work credit" system, whereby sentences were reduced (by two days or more for every day the norm was overfulfilled). Work credits were widely used during the 1930s in correctional-labor camps, colonies, and even in prisons, but an order by the NKVD commissar Beria in the summer of 1939 abolished the credit system and wiped out the workday credits accumulated by prisoners.[53] Beria's justification was that the best prisoners were being released after serving one-half or one-third of their sentences. Beria's order did not quite rule out sentence reductions as rewards for prisoners who attained high productivity results for an extended period, but such exceptional cases were decided by the Special Conference of the NKVD, based on special requests by the camp director and the director of the political department. Beria's order laid out other kinds of rewards, such as better supplies and food, monetary bonuses, meetings with relatives, general improvements in living conditions, and so forth. In general, however, the order represented a tightening of the regime and working conditions in the camps, and it provided for much harsher treatment of inmates who refused to work.

Former inmates confirm that there was no system of workday credits during the 1940s in Norilsk, but ". . . by special decision a sentence could be reduced for excellent work, based on a request by the plant to the government."[54] However, some former inmates report that political prisoners could not receive work credits, though

---

53. In Kokurin/Petrov, it was connected with the speech of Stalin during the meeting of the Presidium of the Supreme Soviet on August 25, 1938. Kokurin/Petrov, Ukaz. soch., "Svobodnaia Mysl," No. 3, 2000, pp. 105–123. Here p. 108.

54. Vintens, *op. cit.*, l. 40–41. The author himself occupied an important position in the chemical laboratory, and for his achievements in modernizing technology, his term of conviction was reduced twice: the first term for a half year, and the second, for one year.

inmates convicted under general articles continued to be awarded credits.[55] We do not know whether the 1939 credit-system ban was partly rescinded later in favor of the "common convicts" or, if rescinded, whether this action was on the initiative of the local camp management. By the end of the 1940s, however, both official documents and inmate memoirs unanimously attest to a turnaround in the policy on workday credits. A joint order of the MVD and the Prosecutor General's Office in July 1948 put into effect instructions on the crediting of workdays to inmates in the Far North construction (Dalstroi) camps.[56] Notably, the July 1948 order gave the right to workday credits to all working inmates, including those sentenced to hard labor, regardless of the length of their sentences, the article under which they were convicted, or how long they had been in the camp. Similar instructions were introduced in late 1948 at projects of the MVD's Main Industrial Construction Administration by Resolution No. 4630-1808ss of the USSR Council of Ministers of December 17, 1948. Both sets of instructions were later gradually applied to many other camps, and they were put into effect in Norillag in May 1950.[57] Within a short period, work credits covered more than half the inmates of Gulag camps and colonies.[58] Three weeks after workday credits were introduced in Norilsk, the Norillag management requested changes, arguing that the specified norms could be overfullfilled only through superhuman efforts in Arctic conditions.[59] V. S. Zverev, the general director of Norilsk,

---

55. Ravdel', *op. cit.*, l. 154, 224. Vintens, *op. cit.*, l. 40.

56. Order of MVD/Office of Public Prosecutor USSR No. 00683/150ss of July 21, 1948, implemented by a resolution of the Council of Ministers USSR No. 1723-688ss of May 22, 1948. See GARF 9414.1. 151: 281.

57. Resolution of Council of Ministers USSR No. 1547-590ss of April 13, 1950 and Order of MVD No. 00287 of May 4, 1950. See GARF 9414.1.151: 281.

58. Zemskov, *op. cit.*, *Sotsiologicheskie Issledovaniia*, No. 7, 1991, pp. 3–16. Here p. 12.

59. By using the workday credit scale established for Dalstroi, the workers in these shops could receive a maximum of .75 of a credit-day for one day worked.

argued for a points system that favored crucial mining and metal-lurgical industries: "It would be absolutely wrong to leave them [mining and metallurgy] in the same category as others, such as construction, power engineers, and mechanics."[60] The management proposed the liberalized credits for metallurgical and enrichment plants shown in Figure 5.5.[61]

These special scales were approved by the Gulag administration, and the Gulag and the Prosecutor General's Office jointly drew up a draft directive to give these proposals legal force in August 1950,[62] though the document itself wasn't adopted until the following year, in the fall of 1951.[63] The delay was not significant, since Zverev had already put his proposed workday-credits scale into practice at Norillag.[64] Zverev's action indicates the freedom the director of a large camp had in making decisions about organizing the inmates' labor. In these decisions, the management of Norillag was obviously spurred by its own stake in creating more effective methods of motivating prison workers. Former inmates confirm that the work-day-credits system came into wide use in the early 1950s.[65]

The same applied to mining operations, where more than 90 percent of workers were in multifunction brigades; the best among them were unable, to all intents and purposes, to fulfill the norms to more than 125 to 130 percent, and accordingly, they would not have been able to get more than one day of credit. The engineering personnel in the plant's metallurgical shops would not have been able to get more than .5 of a credit-day, since the lack of individual norms meant that the awarding of credits by this scale would have depended on the fulfillment of the nickel pro-duction plan set for the entire plant. At that point, however, nickel production had never gone more than 4 percent over the plan in the plant's entire history.

60. GARF 9414.1.151: 285–286, 289.
61. GARF 9414.1.151: 286–287, 290.
62. GARF 9414.1.151: 297–298.
63. GARF 9414.1.151: 299–300.
64. GARF 9414.1.151: 290.
65. Rubinshteyn, *op. cit.*, l. 188–189; Numerov, *op. cit.*, l. 402.

Figure 5.5   Liberalized Credits for Metallurgical and Enrichment Plants

For fulfillment of monthly norms	Prisoners working in mining enterprises
From 100% to 105%	1.5 days
From 106% to 110%	1.75
From 111% to 115%	2
From 116% to 120%	2.5
121% or more	3
For fulfillment of the plan	*Engineers*
At 100%	Up to 2 days
For fulfillment of the plan and all technical-economic targets (unit cost, productivity, input coefficients, accident rate, etc.)	Up to 3 days
For fulfillment of monthly norms	*Ordinary prisoners*
From 100% to 105%	1.5 days
From 106% to 115%	1.75
From 116% to 125%	2
From 126% to 135%	2.5
136% or more	3

MONEY WAGES AND BONUSES

Gulag camps also paid inmates differentiated monetary payments for work performed. Throughout the 1940s, administrative reports referred to these payments as "monetary rewards" and "monetary bonus remuneration." The term "wages" was used occasionally but was not introduced officially until 1950. Before 1950, payments were made in the form of supplemental bonuses. The 1939 "Provisional Instructions on Procedures for Inmates in Correctional Labor Camps" required that bonuses be credited to the inmate's personal account up to a monthly upper limit. Inmates could also be given personal cash, totaling no more than one hundred rubles

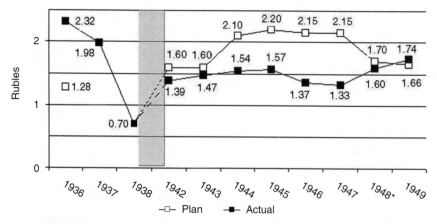

Figure 5.6   Monetary Incentive Fund of Norilsk Complex and Its Usage (Average Monetary Payments per Prisoner Worker per Day, in Rubles)
Source: GARF 9414.1.854: 57, 80; 968: 24–26; 969: 10; 1118: 24; 8361.1.40: 42ob.; 56: 40; 71: 56; 95: 101; 101: 156; 125: 152ob.; 155: 140; 174: 98.

a month, subject to the approval of the division chief. Bonuses and personal cash were issued "piecemeal at different times, in such a manner that the total amount in an inmate's possession [did] not exceed 50 rubles."[66] The 1947 procedures for Gulag inmates spelled out similar terms for monetary rewards for overfulfilling production norms. According to Gulag director V. G. Nasedkin, writing in 1947, inmates could receive cash amounts of not more than 150 rubles at one time. Any sums over this amount were credited to the inmate's account and were paid out as previously issued cash was spent.[67]

Figure 5.6 shows monetary payments per man-day worked for the period 1936 to 1949 to all inmates working at the Norilsk Integrated Plant. Probably most inmates did not receive bonuses; therefore the average figures are lower than the actual bonuses. Bonuses paid out hovered around two rubles a day, suggesting that

66. Order No. 00889 NKVD of August 2, 1939.
67. GARF 9414.1.77: 28.

the average worker would have to overfulfill norms for fifty days to accumulate the one hundred ruble maximum. The average amount of pay was somewhat higher in 1936 than in subsequent years because of normal overfulfillment and an increase in bonuses for skilled workers. For certain projects, "there was an artificial increase in bonus remuneration for the purpose of accelerating projects of an extremely urgent nature."[68] There were also instances in which "the amounts of work completed were artificially inflated."[69] The larger bonuses for skilled workers graphically show that the first directors of Norilsk[70] were actively and deliberately using monetary rewards as incentives at the start of operations. In 1937, the over-expenditure of the monetary-reward fund was viewed as a problem because even a small overfulfillment of output norms by individual groups of workers could cause large increases in bonuses, which would raise the bonus-remuneration fund for fulfillment of the cap-ital-projects plan.[71] Norilsk management drew up new rates "to lower the growth of bonus remuneration for overfulfillment of norms" and introduced "bonus bread." Four hundred grams of bread were moved from the basic allotment to bonus bread issued in place of money bonuses.[72] These and later measures drove down expenditures on money rewards.[73] The Norilsk plant's 1937 report raises some doubt about how reliably money was managed inside the camp: "Accounts of inmate depositors were managed in 1937 by the divisions themselves, which caused numerous abuses, both

68. GARF 9414.1.854: 12.

69. Ibid.

70. The first chief of Norilsk construction and of Norillag, V. Z. Matveev, was arrested and replaced by A. P. Zaveriagin in April 1938.

71. GARF 9414.1.968: 24–25. Note: Apparently, this practice of monetary motivation calculation was not in use in reality because the costs for prisoners' support were lower than planned for nearly every year during this period. Figure 5.6 shows that the situation was the same for premium pay.

72. GARF 9414.1.968: 25.

73. GARF 9414.1.969: 10.

on the part of workers and on the part of accounting employees."[74]
Monetary rewards paid out in the 1940s, especially in the second
half of the decade, were lower than planned amounts, even though
the Norilsk plant was fulfilling and overfulfilling its norms. In 1948
the planned amount was changed to a more realistic, lower figure.
From the plant management's perspective, bonuses were part of the
expenditures on man-days of work in production. Managers under
pressure to lower production costs reduced bonuses as a convenient
means of lowering costs. Norilsk plant data show that savings on
"monetary rewards" in the 1940s kept total expenditures per man-
day of work below planned levels right up until 1948. This effect
was especially noticeable from 1944 to 1947, when savings on other
kinds of costs were disappearing. Since cost economies improved
the general financial capabilities of the enterprise and were cited in
the plant's reports as distinctive achievements, management considered that reducing monetary rewards to cut costs was no less important than the incentive effect of these small bonuses.

The memoirs of former Norilsk inmates do not devote much
space to monetary rewards. While such rewards were mentioned
for Norillag's early period,[75] references become openly skeptical for
the 1940s: "Officially convicts received wages for their work
according to the logs, but the wages never reached them and went
into the pockets of the camp management. Only in 1945 did the
management start to pay out a few crumbs."[76] Rewards for effi-
ciency-improvement proposals submitted by inmates also were triv-
ial. The former inmate A. A. Gayevsky writes: "In May 1942 I was
rewarded for a proposal that yielded an economic benefit totaling
185,100 rubles." Here is the quote from Directive No. 74 of the
NKVD on the Norilsk plant: "For the initiative he has shown,

74. GARF 9414.1.968: 9.
75. See Ravdel', *op. cit.*, l. 115.
76. Assanov, *op. cit.*, l. 11–12.

engineer Gayevsky is to be awarded a bonus of 100 rubles, with a notation made in his personal file, and he is to receive engineers' meals starting 1 June."[77] Judging from Gayevsky's account, the engineer's meal was more significant than the one hundred rubles.

As the 1940s ended, two resolutions ("Pursuant to USSR Council of Ministers Resolutions No. 4293-1703ss of 20 November 1948 and No. 1065-376ss of 13 March 1950") introduced wages for Gulag inmates.[78] Wages were officially introduced to Gulag camps (excluding special camps) by the MVD decree of April 1, 1950.[78] Prisoner wages were based on rates in corresponding civilian sectors, but with appropriate reductions. Inmates received only a small part of their wages in cash after the deduction of food, clothing costs, and income taxes.[80] After these deductions, inmate cash wages were not to be less than 10 percent of their total earnings. Progressive piecework and other bonuses for free workers at MVD enterprises were also applied to prisoners. Inmate administrative and managerial personnel received 50 to 70 percent of the pay of free workers in equivalent jobs.

By directly linking Gulag wages to the civilian economy, inmate wages followed the principles of wage differentiation in the economy at large. These principles included the use of piece rates and bonuses to motivate the fulfillment of production norms; higher pay in such high-priority branches as coal, gold mining, and metallurgy; higher wages for qualified and skilled workers; and higher wages for workers in production as against secondary and auxiliary pro-

77. See memoirs of A. A. Geyevsky on website of Krasnoiarsk Society "Memorial" (http://memorial.krsk.ru/memuar/mgaew.htm).

78. Zemskov, "GULAG (Istoriko-Sotsiologicheskiy Aspekt)," *Sotsiologicheskie Issledovania*, 1991, No. 7, pp. 11–12.

79. See also 9401.4.2693: 177. In reality the mention of ". . . work experience of camps and colonies where prisoners received wages . . ." in this decree indicates that in some camps wages may have been paid earlier."

80. This means that bonuses given to separate groups of workers were not considered.

duction. Prisoners who were temporarily excused from work because of illness or other reasons were not credited with wages, but their food and clothing costs were not withheld. Certified disabled prisoners used in piecework were paid according to prisoners' piecework rates for the work that they actually completed.

The introduction of wages for Norillag inmates created financial problems because the MVD order required that cash wages be paid from the authorized appropriation without an allocation of supplemental funds. The Gulag's metallurgy administration, under which Norilsk fell, reported "inevitable difficulties in the camps' work during this transitional period" and significant deviations "between the authorized estimates of the revenues and expenditures of correctional-labor camps and actual results."[81] Camps such as Norilsk attempted to close the financial gap by cutting "food and clothing allowances as compared with estimates," but these cutbacks "did not offset the increase in wages paid out, since wages at a number of camps were paid out in increased amounts due to the overfulfillment of production norms."[82] A 1952 inspection report on Norillag, however, points out some positive results: "The changeover of inmates to wages was a major incentive for most inmates to raise productivity."[83] The deputy director of Norillag expressed a similar view in a letter dated June 5, 1952, saying that certain groups of inmates, especially in the skilled vocations, were working much more efficiently because of the introduction of wages.[84]

Figure 5.7A shows the distribution of money wages in 1952 for the entire contingent of Norillag's working inmates. The average wage per worker (credited as cash) was about 225 rubles. Because of higher wages in the metallurgical industry, Norillag wages were

81. GARF 9401.4.2693: 177.
82. GARF 9401.4.2693: 178.
83. GARF 9414.1.642: 80.
84. GARF 8361.1.305: 10.

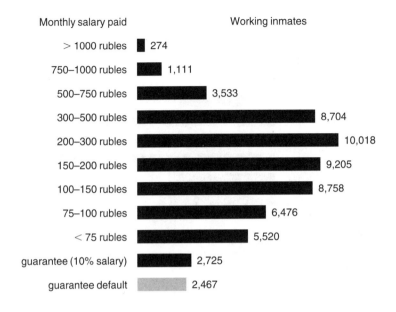

Figure 5.7A   Average Number of Working Inmates by Monthly Average Salary Paid in 1952
Source: GARF 9414.1.174: 34ob.

higher than at other camps. At the same time, the average wage of a qualified worker in the civilian economy stood at 1,465 rubles a month in mining, 1,343 rubles in ferrous metallurgy, and 651 rubles in garments and shoes.[85] Thus Norilsk inmates received about one-third the pay of the lowest-paid civilian workers and about 15 percent of the pay of workers in comparable jobs, although inmates did receive "free" housing and food. Figure 5.7A shows considerable dispersion of money wages: while almost five thousand inmates

85. This takes into account prisoners who were deprived of wages. The data, however, do not allow calculating precisely the average wage, and thus it is necessary to proceed from possible error in this estimation in the range of 5 to 10 percent. For 1953 civilian wages, see V. P. Popov, *Ekonomicheskaia Politika Sovetskogo Gosudarstva. 1946–1953* (Moscow: Tambov, 2000), p. 65.

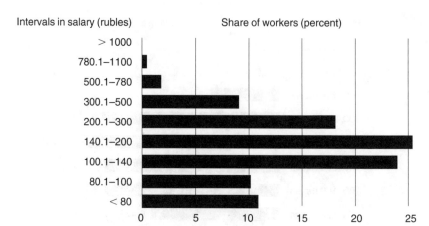

Figure 5.7B   Monthly Salary Distribution of Industrial Workers in USSR, 1934
Source: A. Bergson, The Structure of Soviet Wages. A Study in Socialist Economics
(Cambridge: Harvard University Press, 1946), 228.

received more than five hundred rubles a month, more than eight
thousand received less than 75 rubles.[86] Figure 5.7B, which shows
the 1934 distribution of industrial workers' wages in the USSR,
yields a similar level of differentiation in the "noncamp" economy.[87]
Such substantial differentiation in inmate wages shows that the
Gulag, like the civilian economy, held out the prospect of higher
monetary earnings to motivate labor. Those who worked well
received relatively large material rewards; those who did not,
received little.

Accounts of former prisoners describe the effect of wages in
Norilsk. Cheburekin, a former Norillag inmate, wrote that wages
were introduced for inmates "at northern rates, but 30 percent
lower than for free workers. They withheld only for 'room and

86. We conclude that prisoners who received a guaranteed 10 percent from
payroll salary accounting are also in this category. Prisoners who were totally
deprived of wages are not included in this sum.
87. Unfortunately, we do not have reliable data about the distribution of salaries of industrial employees in the USSR at the beginning of the 1950s.

board,' and the rest went into my bank account. I could take up to 250 rubles a month for my expenses. . . . I received 1,200 rubles a month, and after all the deductions something was left over, and accumulated in the account. Some professional drivers . . . earned up to 5,000 a month!"[88] A. A. Gayevsky, an engineer, remembered the following: "When I was released from the camp in 1947, I got back 2,561 rubles and 63 kopeks of the money that I had earned, and I was issued a cotton blanket, a lumpy mattress, a sheet and a pillowcase."[89] After Gayevsky received his certificate of release, which stated that he was to go to his "chosen" place of residence— the settlement of Norilsk in Krasnoyarsk Krai (which wasn't yet a city in 1947)—he remained at the plant in the same job, though in the new capacity of free worker. But since his sentence had stripped him of his rights for five years, he did not receive the benefits for workers in the Far North.[90]

CONCLUSIONS

Norilsk was one of the highest-priority Gulag operations, shown by the steady growth of prison labor in Norilsk despite fluctuations in the total camp population. Despite Norilsk's harsh natural conditions, Norilsk prisoners were less likely to die than prisoners were elsewhere, and there were more free workers in Norilsk than in other camps. Norilsk appeared to follow general Gulag regulations closely for hours and days worked, but labor effort was dictated more by production requirements than by rules (for example, harsh weather rules were often ignored). Norilsk's best workers could earn work credits to reduce their prison terms, though sentence reductions for good work were granted only as an exception before

88. Cheburekin, *op. cit.,* l. 21.
89. See: A. A. Gaevskiy, *op. cit.*
90. Ibid.

1950. The fact that Norilsk put its own work-credit system into effect before receiving central approval suggests that Gulag managers had considerable authority. Norilsk, like other camps, relied more on material incentives as time passed, but the need to cover monetary bonuses from general cash funds limited bonuses to token amounts before 1950. In 1950 Norilsk inmates were placed on a wage system, patterned after the civilian wage system, but Norilsk inmates appeared to earn less than half of comparable wages in the civilian sector. The Norilsk archives show that "free" workers were far from free. Most were former inmates, denied the right to leave Norilsk. After completing their sentences, they received higher pay, more privileges, and occupied a middle ground between convict and truly free labor.

Magadan and the Economic History of Dalstroi in the 1930s

David Nordlander

AMONG A HOST of issues, the history of the Gulag raises several interrelated political and economic questions that address the essence of Stalin's industrialization campaign in the 1930s. Above all, the question arises of whether the labor camps were created mainly as repositories for the victims of political repression or whether they served the larger goal of economic necessity in the Soviet Union. Phrased another way, were the pace and scale of arrests shaped by industrial goals, or were they merely a function of political interests throughout the Stalin era? The question of the economic efficiency of forced labor is also important because it addresses the productive capacity of Stalinism. An analysis of Dalstroi, which was headquartered in the Russian Far Eastern city of Magadan, is instrumental in understanding the ebb and flow and relative balance of political and economic imperatives in the 1930s.

Before such an investigation, however, there is a need for some background on the economic history of Dalstroi. This penal agency constituted the largest entity in the entire labor camp system; its acronym Dalstroi stood for Far Northern Construction Trust (Glavnoe upravlenie stroitel'stvo Dalnego Severa NKVD SSSR), a euphemism for a ruthless organization whose wide array of functions made it the overlord in the Soviet northeast. Sandwiched between the Pacific and Arctic Oceans, Dalstroi in time came to administer more than 130 camp facilities in a territory covering nearly 3 million square kilometers and stretching to the tip of the Bering Strait. Encompassing the northern right bank of the Lena River, the Indigirka and Kolyma Rivers, the Chukotka Peninsula, and a section of northern Kamchatka, this region formed a landmass bigger than that of Western Europe. Dalstroi was also a favorite child of the NKVD, the People's Commissariat of Internal Affairs, which succeeded the Cheka and OGPU as the main organization of the secret police in 1934. As a result, this Gulag subdivision possessed numerous resources to carry out its mission as a branch of that legendary security agency.[1]

For the USSR, the primary value of Dalstroi rested upon gold. Since this rare mineral provided the Soviet government with an irreplaceable commodity for foreign exchange and further economic development, Magadan in particular proved significant to the Kremlin. The Politburo and NKVD made a hefty investment in Dalstroi while assigning it ever-ascending production quotas throughout the Stalin era. As a result, this agency played a significant but hidden part in the national economy. From the perspective of Moscow, camp inmates were tools for attaining mining records. Since Stalin saw Dalstroi as the means for tapping some of the richest mineral resources in the USSR, party propaganda urged the Gulag workforce to ship copious amounts of gold to Kremlin coffers. The refrain trumpeted by the state trust echoed a clear mission: "We Must Give the Party Double the Amount of Metal as Last Year."[2]

---

1. For a brief outline of regional history, see Aleksandr Kozlov, *Magadan: Konspekt Proshlogo* (Magadan: Magadanskoe knizhnoe izdatel'stvo, 1989).

2. GAMO (*Gosudarstvennyi arkhiv Magadanskoi oblasti*—State Archive of the Magadan Region), f. r-23s, op. 1, d. 12, l. 4.

Over the years, the Soviet economy benefited enormously from Dalstroi's prison operations. While the productivity of forced labor proved low, the state trust achieved output figures that pleased Stalin and boosted the anemic hard currency reserves of the USSR. Considering the value of gold, the large quantities mined by Dalstroi in the mid-1930s became a financial boon to Moscow and paid to a certain extent the investment costs of the regional camps. For that matter, the state trust produced economic returns far above projected values. Economic achievement came as no small feat, however, since prison bosses often had to wrestle with equipment deficits as well as with incompetent, incapacitated, and emaciated prisoners. Such was certainly the case during the tenure of the first Dalstroi director, E. P. Berzin. But excavation figures for gold nonetheless more than doubled each year from 1932 to 1936, causing official displays of admiration and praise from the Kremlin and a further increase in regional investment. The returns from 1936 so excited A. P. Serebrovskii, an industrial commissar, that he erroneously rhapsodized: "Never, in the most feverish years of the capitalist gold rush that included all the metal taken out of Alaska, did a territory give as much gold as that produced this year by the new Kolyma region."[3]

In the early Stalin era, economic rather than political needs were paramount and therefore determined the fate of prisoners sent to Dalstroi. Soviet authorities in the early 1930s were not yet ostracizing and humiliating inmates because the focus in the Gulag was concentrated on industrial issues. Data for mineral production show commercial benefits resulting from the employment of Gulag inmates in the region: between 1932 and 1934, Dalstroi raised its annual mining totals from 511 to 5,515 kilograms of pure gold.[4]

3. See Kozlov, "Pervyi Direktor," *Politicheskaia Agitatsiia*, No. 18 (September 1988).

4. GAMO, f. r-23ss, op. 1, d. 5, ll. 14-20.

Although this amount was not huge, the tenfold increase presaged a bountiful future. Such returns would prove significant for Stalin's programs, since international gold sales became one of the chief means of raising foreign exchange to pay for the Soviet industrialization effort. Financial incentives provided the impetus for Dalstroi's birth and evolution, a motivating force that would not be matched until political considerations began to dominate events in the late 1930s.

But state priorities in the Berzin era and throughout the early 1930s focused on labor exploitation rather than on political destruction. To achieve its industrial plans in the region, Dalstroi began importing ever-larger contingents of inmates. In June 1932, the penal ships *Kashirstroi* and *Dneprostroi* arrived from Vladivostok, with the first large prison boatloads arriving in Nagaevo Bay. By the end of that year, the Gulag in Magadan processed 9,928 prisoners to different camp enterprises.[5] Even the composition of these penal drafts showed that Stalin's first, more practical aim concentrated on the economic development of the territory. The overwhelming majority of the original inmates were not "politicals" but common criminals, with the rest including some "dekulakized" peasants from Soviet agricultural regions.[6] Political prisoners were the least productive class of prisoner but made up only a small percentage of camp totals until after the onset of the Great Purges.

As inmate totals grew, Dalstroi spread its prisoners to mining and industrial sites throughout the region. Though Soviet authorities first built camps along the Okhotsk coastline and then along the Kolyma River, Gulag branch camps in time extended westward to the Lena River and eastward to the Chukotka Peninsula at the farthest tip of the country. In 1932, however, camp officials concentrated prisoners in and around Magadan, since most construc-

5. GAMO, f. r-23ss, op. 1, d. 6, l. 55.
6. Kozlov, "Oni Byli Pervymi," *Reklamnaia Gazeta*, March 14, 1989, 4.

tion activity in the early years focused on building the city itself and the highway leading to the site of gold strikes in the interior. Penal ships made regular runs during the summer and fall from Vladivostok to the port of Nagaevo, where prisoners transferred to a transit station for registration and dispatch to work assignments. To accommodate the projects with greatest labor needs, Berzin established camp zones throughout the new metropolis and surrounding countryside, an area that became the initial base of the Gulag along the shores of the North Pacific. By 1934, the state trust had also established hard labor camps at the rich mineral deposits to the north of Magadan to expand the territory's gold operations.[7]

The Soviet government provided Dalstroi with every possible means to complete its mission, including ever-larger prison contingents that soon formed the predominant labor base in all trust enterprises. Statistics reveal the overwhelming reliance of the regional Gulag on prisoners, a reliance that persisted throughout the history of the state trust. Freely hired personnel composed on average only 15 percent of the total workforce, while the remaining 85 percent consisted of prisoners. Between 1932 and 1934, regional labor figures for both free and involuntary workers nearly tripled, from 13,053 to 35,995. Prisoner counts for the same years rose from 9,928 to 32,304, an even faster rate of increase that at times showed prisoner averages approaching 90 percent of the total workforce.[8] Changing little throughout the 1930s, this ratio accentuated the unusual problems in creating a viable workforce for Magadan. Without the "human capital" provided by the Gulag, industrial development would not have proceeded in the territory. Dalstroi's experience framed earlier debates in the Politburo, Sovnarkom (Council of People's Commissars), and Narkomtrud (People's Commissariat of Labor) on the potentially crippling labor shortage

7. Kozlov, "'Zolotoi' Iubilei," *Politicheskaia Agitatsiia* (June 1989), 21–25.
8. GAMO, f. r-23ss, op. 1, d. 6, l. 55.

throughout the region, a problem that Stalin had resolved in his expansion of the Gulag network through the resolution "On the Use of Prison Labor" in June 1929.[9] Magadan can be seen as a textbook study demonstrating the economic reasons behind the widespread exploitation of camp inmates in the Stalin era.[10]

In economic goals, Dalstroi exceeded nearly all quotas set by the Soviet government during the second Five-Year Plan (1933–37). Economic output more than rose in proportion to the equipment and "human capital" sent to Dalstroi. From the total of 32,304 prisoners for 1934, prisoner numbers rose again to 44,601 in 1935 and to 62,703 by the close of 1936.[11] In relative terms, gold-mining statistics exceeded the influx of prisoners. Production returns in Magadan rose exponentially for each of the first several years of camp operations. From the extraction of 5,515 kilograms of chemically pure gold in 1934, Berzin more than doubled production to 14,458 kg in 1935 and twice as much again to 33,360 kg by the end of 1936.[12] To place these statistics in a national context, the Soviet Union overall mined only 13,215 kg of gold in 1927 and 1928. Moreover, Dalstroi's production alone by the mid-1930s almost matched total tsarist gold-mining figures from the years before World War I.[13]

In response to the economic attainments of the Gulag in Magadan, Stalin and Molotov sent annual commendatory telegrams, such

9. RGASPI (Rossiiskii gosudarstvennyi arkhiv sotsial'no-politicheskoi istorii—Russian State Archive of Social and Political History), f. 17, op. 3, d. 746, l. 11 (Politburo protocols).

10. For more on the economic ramifications of Gulag labor in the region, see S. M. Mel'nikov, "Dal'stroi: Stranitsy Istorii," *Kolyma*, nos. 9–10 (1993): 46.

11. For the annual totals of Gulag prisoners within the state trust during these years, see GAMO, f. r-23ss, op. 1, d. 6, l. 55.

12. For annual gold production figures for Dalstroi at this time, see reference note 11, f. r-23ss, op. 1, d. 5, ll. 14–20.

13. For comparative statistics on earlier tsarist and Soviet gold-mining totals, see Mel'nikov, "Dal'stroi: Stranitsy Istorii," *Kolyma*, nos. 9–10 (1993): 44–47.

as the following in 1936: "We congratulate the workers and leadership of the trust Dalstroi upon fulfillment of the program for gold-mining, and send Bolshevik greetings."[14] Berzin had received the highest state honor in the preceding year when the Soviet government awarded him an Order of Lenin in the Kremlin for outstanding service in surpassing target figures for gold production, an accolade also awarded to his leading deputies, Z. A. Almazov and A. N. Pemov.[15] Several other subordinates concurrently won citations, all of which were highlighted nationally on the front page of *Pravda*. The most intriguing citations went to a handful of Dalstroi prisoners, who received early release *(dosrochnoe osvobozhdenie)* for their part in achieving the lionized results. From the standpoint of central authorities, the future appeared bright with promise for these regional officials "at the vanguard of socialist labor."[16]

For all the honors, Berzin and his assistants knew that their careers, if not their lives, depended on the unbroken continuation of such exploits. Since the prosperity of Dalstroi, as of other subdivisions of the Gulag, relied on the sweat of prisoners, camp administrators focused on ways to motivate their inmates and stimulate production. Unlike civilian managers, however, prison bosses could not make use of normal incentives. They could reward inmate output with higher rations or small material inducements but were otherwise hamstrung in their options. Berzin and other Gulag chiefs thus turned to ideological campaigns to inspire and cajole inmates. While having fulminated in years past on the heroic efforts needed for the "opening of the Far North" to civilization, party rhetoric in the mid-1930s highlighted new slogans that redefined the goals of public life in Magadan. With increasing regularity, Berzin sought

14. GAMO, f. r-23s, op. 1, d. 26, ll. 26-27.
15. RGASPI 17.3.961: 44–46.
16. For the national recognition of these awards, see *Pravda*, March 23, 1935, 1.

to animate the Dalstroi workforce by using the mottoes of "socialist competition" *(sotsialisticheskoe sorevnovanie)* and "shock-work" *(udarnichestvo)*, both of which emphasized attaining production records through honest rivalry, for the good of the state and the redemption of inmates. By the fall of 1935, the Stakhanov campaign augmented this effort and began to grip Magadan, thus raising the production stakes even higher. Lacking the corporate competition of the capitalist West, Soviet and Gulag institutions trumpeted such slogans as "socialist competition," "shock-work," and "Stakhanovism" to drive up labor productivity.[17]

But Stalin remained the master of cynical pragmatism. In contrast to the public protestations of Soviet life, the Kremlin boss was obsessed with economic production and political control. Reflecting his interest in Soviet industrialization, Stalin referred to Magadan in private as the administrative capital of prison camps in a gold-producing region. Both he and his assistants spoke of "inmate productivity," "norms," "quotas," and "output," but *never* of the supposed benefits from the "opening of the Far North" to civilization and modernity or of the redemptive power of labor campaigns.[18] From the perspective of the Kremlin, Magadan existed as the center of a domestic colony based on slave labor. While constantly pestering Berzin about industrial plans and the proper use of Gulag conscripts, neither Stalin nor Molotov ever wrote to the Dalstroi boss about the ethereal goals of Marxism-Leninism that peppered regional newspapers. In one communication, Stalin issued a resolution through the Council of People's Commissars, counter-

---

17. For more on Stakhanovism and related campaigns, see Lewis H. Siegelbaum, *Stakhanovism and the Politics of Productivity* (New York: Cambridge University Press, 1985). For an analysis of the use of such terms and their role in the camp economy, see G. M. Ivanova, *GULAG v Sisteme Totalitarnogo Gosudarstva* (Moscow: Moskovskii Obshchestvennyi Nauchnyi Fond, 1997), 92–93.

18. For one representation of such practical Kremlin concerns, see RGASPI 17.3.888: 38–46.

signed by Molotov, that informed Berzin of specific trust investment figures and the current price of gold.[19]

Underneath the propaganda campaigns, signs of these practical interests appeared with regularity in Magadan. The composition of the original penal drafts reflected the utilitarian concerns of state. By the end of 1932 these drafts numbered nearly ten thousand inmates, replete with kulaks and "wreckers" who offered practical farming and engineering skills valuable to camp administrators. In particular, the ten prisoners who arrived with Berzin on the S. S. *Sakhalin* were industrial specialists who provided Dalstroi with an expertise crucial for setting up operations. Following in the wake of the Shakhty and Industrial Union Trials in 1928, which had begun the party assault on specialists accused of sabotage and treason against the USSR, the Soviet government repressed many scientific personnel alleged to be "bourgeois" agents engaged in covert activities.[20] Arrested under the charge of "wrecking" (*vreditel'skaia deiatel'nost'*), the most common accusation against engineers in the late 1920s and early 1930s—many of these specialists had played an important part in establishing a technical foundation for the Gulag.[21]

Analysis of the specialists sent as the first inmates to Dalstroi reveals that the original show trials, regardless of public questions of guilt or innocence, took aim at technicians who were desperately needed in remote regions of the USSR but who could never be recruited voluntarily. Seven of these first prisoners in Magadan had

19. GAMO, f. r-23ss, op. 1, d. 1, l. 186.

20. For an analysis of the Shakhty Trial, see Hiroaki Kuromiya, *Stalin's Industrial Revolution: Politics and Workers, 1928–1932* (Cambridge: Cambridge University Press, 1988), 12–17. For more on the first industrial show trials, see Kendall Bailes, *Technology and Society under Lenin and Stalin* (Princeton: Princeton University Press, 1978), chapter 3.

21. The technical specialists arrested as "wreckers" lived in the relatively open camp zones and enjoyed at least a measure of mobility unknown in later years. See Kozlov, "U Istokov Sevvostlaga," *Kolyma*, 1992 (no. 12): 27–32.

long-standing experience in the mining industry, two were labor organization experts, and one had served as a hydraulic engineer for many years. Dalstroi urgently needed these kinds of specialists, as did other Gulag entities across the USSR, a need that no doubt influenced arrest patterns of the period. At the same time, the patterns of employment of specialists in the labor camps of the early 1930s also unveil other realities of the Soviet penal system that help distinguish this period from the tragedies that occurred when the Stalin Terror reached full swing in 1937 and 1938.[22]

Spawned by political considerations, the Great Purges in Magadan, as elsewhere in the USSR, produced deleterious consequences. Berzin was arrested in late 1937 and replaced by a new and much harsher camp boss, K. A. Pavlov. The new prison administration arrested most of Berzin's subordinates as well. Soon afterward, economic production tailed off for Dalstroi as previous growth rates began a steady decline. Since the Gulag in Magadan had received a huge influx of prisoners at the time of the Stalin Terror, such a decline in mining output probably appeared glaring to Soviet leaders who had expected the opposite. By the end of the 1930s in the northeastern region alone, more than 163,000 inmates slaved at camp enterprises as Dalstroi finally achieved an adequate number of prison laborers for fulfilling state plans. But the incarceration or execution of many specialists, who had acquired expertise through years of work for the Gulag, exacted a heavy toll, especially since their replacements often did not have commensurate skills. "Cadre leapfrog," in which employees stumbled over each other through the revolving door of the prisons, caused havoc and made it increasingly difficult to fulfill the goals of the Five-Year Plan.[23]

22. Kozlov, "Oni Byli Pervymi," 4.
23. In economic impact, the events in Magadan during the Great Purges support the contentions of Alec Nove about the negative effects of the Stalin Terror on the industrial output and fulfillment of state plans caused by repressions against technical cadre. See Alec Nove, *An Economic History of the USSR, 1917–1991*

By late September 1938, even local Gulag bosses began to appreciate the effect of this turnover of specialists. Having lost a number of qualified experts over the preceding nine months, Dalstroi scrambled to replace essential personnel. The political imperatives of the age had eclipsed the rational necessities of the Soviet state, an imbalance that had to be redressed since it threatened economic output. On 28 September, the deputy Gulag director in Magadan, A. A. Khodyrev, authorized the creation of a mining technical college that would train a new generation of geologists, prospectors, and engineers to replace those who had been purged. As a reflection of how deeply the Great Terror had touched the region, depopulating it of a talented cadre, officials underscored the need to seek student candidates not only from among trustworthy civilian staff but from demobilized Red Army soldiers, low-level camp guards, and even residents of local native communities.[24] The Kremlin paid a high price for its untrammeled search for spies and saboteurs in 1937 and 1938, since the industrial capacity of agencies like Dalstroi began to slip along with the loss of its "human capital."

The greatest index for the drop of productivity in the Magadan region at this time can be seen in Gulag inmate totals and gold-mining statistics. Though Berzin had produced exponential returns for gold in a ratio which exceeded the gradual inflow of prisoners, Pavlov presided over a contraction of output despite the greater number of inmates at his disposal. In 1936, 62,703 inmates mined 33,360 kilograms of chemically pure gold. Fewer than 2 inmates on average were thus required for producing one kilogram of gold. In 1939, 163,475 inmates mined 66,314 kilograms of pure gold. At this time, the regional Gulag required 2.5 inmates for yielding one

(London: Penguin Books, 1992), 259–60. See also R. Medvedev, *Let History Judge: The Origins and Consequences of Stalinism*, ed. and trans. George Shriver (New York: Columbia University Press, 1989), 456.

    24. GAMO, f. r-23s, op. 1, d. 37, l. 71.

kilogram of gold. Prison rolls grew significantly by about 70,000 between 1938 and 1939, from 93,978 to 163,475. The amount of gold increased by only 4,000 kilograms, however, from 62,008 to 66,314. At the height of the Stalin Terror in Magadan, the significant inflow of prisoners led to only one additional kilogram of gold for every 17 new inmates. Such poor production totals show that the political fury of the Great Purges undermined the initial economic raison d'être of the Gulag and may help explain why the Terror came to an abrupt halt after less than two years. By 1939, the USSR could no longer afford the bloodletting.[25]

To counteract these negative trends, the Kremlin pumped additional funding and resources into Dalstroi just to meet plan goals. Both secret police chiefs Nikolai Ezhov and Lavrenty Beria pressured numerous agencies to ship new equipment and technical supplies to Magadan, where camp authorities continued to struggle with a deficit of materials. Shortly before his ouster in 1938, Ezhov requested that Sovnarkom force the state bank (Gosbank) to provide more funds so that Dalstroi could upgrade much of its outdated technology in an attempt to close the mining gap.[26] Moscow, moreover, agreed to spend nearly 2 million rubles to repair two prison transport ships from Magadan, the *Dalstroi* and the *Dzhurma*, which had been heavily damaged by ice on the Sea of Okhotsk.[27] In December 1938, Sovnarkom even issued a resolution providing Dalstroi with an upper limit of funding, as needed, through July 1, 1939.[28] Despite intragovernmental complaints that NKVD mismanagement was the source of camp problems, the rapid action of the Kremlin reflected both the sense of urgency caused by Dalstroi's economic failings in 1937 and 1938 and the need to reorient the

25. Ibid., f. 23ss, op. 1, d. 5, l. 14.
26. GARF (Gosudarstvennyi arkhiv Rossiiskoi Federatsii—State Archive of the Russian Federation), f. 5446, op. 23a, d. 61, ll. 7–8.
27. Ibid., d. 92, ll. 11–17.
28. Ibid., d. 178, l. 1.

state trust for a more productive future. Until the Great Terror ended, however, the earlier levels of industrial growth did not return, and Magadan remained in the grip of political chaos.

Although eliciting definitive reasons for either the beginning or ending of the Great Purges may be beyond the pale of scholarship, the economic standing of Dalstroi by the middle of 1939 offers clues to the ending of this epoch. The Stalin Terror had mangled the productive capability of the northeastern trust. As industrial considerations fell victim to political mandates, the Kremlin may have reaped intangible benefits but could not altogether ignore the harmful effect of the Great Terror on economic affairs. The impressive mining output achieved by Dalstroi under Berzin evaporated in 1938 and 1939. The exponential growth rates of the first six years could not be sustained by the trust administration under Berzin's successor, who presided over a precipitous decline in the recovery of gold and other minerals. In industrial yield, the Gulag in Magadan did not recover from the twin impact of the Stalin Terror and World War II until the late 1940s. Even then, it never approached the successes attained by Berzin, who in retrospect proved to be the most capable manager in the history of Dalstroi. Although Stalin may have desired the removal of officials like Berzin for reasons of political reliability, in time Stalin came to appreciate the concomitant loss of administrative and economic competence. As the experience of Magadan reveals, the Great Purges carried a price that the Kremlin may have considered too high by the second half of 1939.

In the meantime, a vicious cycle ensued in which the rhetoric and repression that underwrote regional economic decline increased with every decrease in output. Stalin soon took action to curtail the downward economic spiral of Dalstroi by naming yet another new administration of the state trust under the leadership of I. F. Nikishov. Stalin evidently realized that political methods useful during the Terror would not help in reviving productivity. As had been the case with Berzin's ouster, this reversal in emphasis led to revamping the staff of the local Gulag. In assigning fresh management to Magadan, Stalin reinforced the industrial mission under which Dalstroi had first come to life in the fall of 1931. As a result, the violence of the Great Purges abated in Magadan before the close of 1939 as Dalstroi returned to its previous task of increasing gold recovery in the territory for the eager coffers of the Kremlin. Scarred by the political violence during the Garaninshchina (the local name for the Great Terror in Magadan, after the notorious camp boss, S. N. Garanin), Magadan never returned to what in retrospect seemed the halcyon days of the Berzin era.

But in economic output, the new Dalstroi administration under Nikishov focused on reestablishing earlier rates of industrial production achieved by the state trust under Berzin. In the early 1940s, the return to an emphasis on mining accomplishments implied that Dalstroi officials would again be scrutinized according to financial indices rather than political considerations. Spurred by the threat of war, which caused numerous changes in Gulag activities, economic output began to revive in Magadan.[29] As in the Berzin era, rewards and commendations from the Kremlin were based on the production of record quantities of gold or tin and other industrial achievements. In response to such incentives from above, local Gulag bosses returned Dalstroi operations to the production rates of the early to mid-1930s.[30]

In accord with the practical aims behind the revival of Berzin's industrial heritage, Nikishov received more material and human assistance in his efforts to resuscitate camp operations. Aside from increased funding and equipment, Dalstroi received additional

29. At the same time, Moscow continued to send supplementary materials and funding to Magadan so that Dalstroi could attain these economic goals. See GARF 5446.23a.184: 66–69.
30. As a cornerstone of this industrial revival, rewards for output percolated to all levels of the state trust under Nikishov. See *Sovetskaia Kolyma*, October 4, 1940, 1.

inmates until the beginning of World War II in June 1941. By the end of 1940, Sevvostlag (Northeastern Camps—a prison agency subservient to Dalstroi) contained 176,685 inmates, a number that fell to 148,301 by the close of 1941 because of the large-scale release and transfer of inmates following the German invasion. But Gulag output nevertheless paralleled Kremlin investments, and Dalstroi mining totals once again approached the levels of the Berzin era. Dalstroi produced 80,028 kilograms of chemically pure gold in 1940 and 75,770 kilograms by the end of 1941. In the tin industry, Dalstroi processed 1,917 tons in 1940 and another 3,226 tons by the end of 1941.[31]

As a reflection of such practicality, Nikishov ordered a broad review of inmate files and granted a general amnesty for many inmates, particularly specialists, who had recently been imprisoned.[32] Because of the detention of many geologists and engineers throughout the Gulag in 1937 and 1938, camp bosses like Nikishov scoured inmate rolls across the USSR for technical personnel considered essential to industrial resuscitation nationwide. Following a superficial review of cases, most of which had been incautiously fabricated and thus were easy to rescind, thousands of technocrats were released from the camps in the early 1940s and returned to their former jobs. The widespread cancellation of sentences from the Great Purges replenished the technicians who had fueled the success of the Berzin period. Besides the return of these specialists to their normal tasks, related policy changes helped reestablish the potential for industrial prosperity in regional camps.[33]

Most important, Nikishov renewed a more rational use of labor, which had been undermined by the Garaninshchina. Following Ber-

31. GAMO, f. r-23ss, op. 1, d. 5, ll. 14–20, 55.
32. See Efimov, "Nachal'nik Dal'stroia I. F. Nikishov," *Kolyma*, no. 11 (1991): 35.
33. Ibid.

zin's ouster in 1937, economic output fell in part because many arrested specialists no longer filled roles related to their expertise. While a few *zek*, or prison, scientists continued to work in their fields, many imprisoned geologists and engineers found themselves slaving at manual tasks that never tapped into their knowledge or capabilities (the famous rocket scientist of Sputnik fame, S. P. Korolev, serves as but one example in Dalstroi). The distrust of inmates often led to their being employed in an irrational way during the Great Purges, an inefficient use of talent that persisted in the camps even under Nikishov because of the deep-seated impulse to humiliate political prisoners. The new Dalstroi chief nonetheless tried to turn this situation around, since it was clear that such attitudes had undermined the productive capability of the regional Gulag. At the same time, Nikishov abolished many of the irrational restrictions placed on former inmates.[34]

In an attempt to reclaim economic growth, Nikishov revived a number of Berzin's initiatives with Moscow's acquiescence. Foremost among these were the material rewards given to prisoners and free civilians alike for superior levels of production. While Pavlov had also used a graduated scale of rations and monetary prizes dependent on output, he had so mangled the range of Berzin's original categories as to undermine their effect in stimulating worker productivity. Nikishov removed the more punitive aspects of Pavlov's program, while petitioning the Kremlin for the early release of prisoners who had performed with distinction. Since such a practice had fallen out of common use in 1937 and 1938, Nikishov's petitions on behalf of prisoners reinvigorated yet another Berzin practice. So too did the shortening of terms for industrious prisoners, who by fulfilling their labor quota in the first years of

---

34. Nikishov's orders in general reflected the more rational purpose of camp administrators in the early 1940s. For example, see GAMO, f. r-23s, op. 1, d. 63, l. 35.

Dalstroi's existence had received added credit for workdays, leading to a reduction of up to half the term of their sentences.[35]

To be fair, production initiatives had not completely disappeared under Pavlov. But although he referred to inmate rewards and on occasion handed them out, they proved ineffective amid the repressive onslaught of the Great Purges. In 1937 and 1938, Dalstroi policy was so punitive toward prisoners arrested under Article 58 that existing material incentives seemed meaningless. Of Pavlov's six inmate categories, in which all rations were based on labor output, only the top two offered even an adequate level of sustenance. Caloric norms fell so low that only "shock-workers" and Stakhanovites had a chance to avoid malnutrition.[36] Although a conscious policy of Soviet authorities was to eliminate "Article 58ers" by attrition, these circumstances undermined production in the Gulag. Overwhelmed by the political calculus of the Great Terror, Pavlov and other camp directors overlooked this problem, even though it harmed economic output. But Dalstroi could not long continue a policy of eliminating political prisoners—a class of inmates that began to compose a high percentage of camp totals. By contrast, Nikishov aimed to revive the successful prisoner inducements from the Berzin era.[37]

Aside from problems caused by the Great Purges, Nikishov had to struggle against the age-old nuisance of Russian inefficiency. While industrial production had fallen off in 1937 and 1938 because of punitive measures, it remained bedeviled by bureaucratic incompetence and shoddy work attitudes. Moreover, perpetual drunkenness among prison guards often resulted in botched assignments,

35. See Efimov, "Nachal'nik Dal'stroia," 35.

36. GAMO, f. r-23s, op. 1, d. 34, ll. 47–48.

37. At the same time, conditions in the camps improved somewhat from the time of the Garaninshchina. But although labeled by some as "relatively humanitarian," they remained grim. See L. Komarova, "Likholet'e," *Magadanskaia pravda*, December 6, 1988.

such as the common misdirection of inmate contingents who never showed up at the proper camp facility.[38] Dalstroi bosses—still limited by ideological blinders, which made them insist on increasing "vigilance" to correct these shortcomings—often proved unable to overcome their continuing troubles. Unlike Pavlov, however, Nikishov instituted several practical measures aimed not only at the "enemy" but also at staff ineptitude, the most glaring deficiency in the state trust. Some of these measures consisted of the most elementary practices, such as requiring camp officers to transmit written lists of prisoners at transfer points so that Gulag officials could trace their captives at all times.[39]

Nikishov also hoped that the revival of serious incentive programs from the Berzin era might help surmount managerial incompetence and promote economic growth. Civilian employees, many of whom had been marginalized (if not arrested) during the Garaninshchina, would again strive for coveted bonuses just as inmates had. As a result, the formerly lionized notions of "socialist competition" returned with full force during the early 1940s. The Nikishov administration even outdid Berzin in spreading the concept of such idealized rivalry into every corner of Gulag activities. Honorific titles and civic recognition once more awaited the victors of these contests, along with prospects for material gain. Voluntary workers won cash prizes or other prizes, such as a gold watch, while prisoners most often received higher rations or even early release. In line with Soviet custom, Nikishov dedicated the new rounds of competition to political events. In December 1940, a contest between miners took place in memory of the Eighteenth Party Con-

38. For one such case, see TsKhSDMO (Tsentr khraneniia sovremennykh dokumentov Magadanskoi oblasti—Center for the Preservation of the Modern Documents of the Magadan Region), f. 1, op. 2, d. 163, ll. 1–3.

39. OSF ITs UVD (Otdelenie spetsial'nykh fondov, Informatsionnyi tsentr Upravleniia vnutrennykh del—Department of Special Funds, Information Center for the Administration of Internal Affairs), f. 11, op. 1, d. 2, ll. 1–2.

gress. While the results were probably fabricated by the media to trumpet inmate "promises" of overfulfilling labor norms, camp bosses aimed to create an atmosphere that would elevate production in the camps. With the goal of attaining annual mining targets, many Gulag competitions came in the month of December in order to meet all industrial plans before the end of the year.[40]

Aside from increasing economic output, these campaigns offered the opportunity to carry out propaganda both inside and outside the camps. Although kept deliberately uninformed of most political affairs by camp administrators, prisoners at the beginning of the 1940s often found themselves compelled to dedicate the over-fulfillment of plan quotas to specific resolutions, such as those of the Eighteenth Party Congress. Because of the tight restriction of information inside the Gulag, the mechanical parroting of recent party decisions accompanied bouts of "socialist competition" and allowed for the spread of carefully worded Soviet precepts to the inmate population. Despite their ignorance of Soviet life beyond the barbed wire, however, successful prisoners were said to have "warmly accepted the resolutions of the Central Committee from the Eighteenth All-Union Party Congress and expressed their love and devotion to the party and government, including the people's leader, Comrade Stalin."[41] Even though most inmates viewed all prison campaigns with profound cynicism, they played along for the material advantages.

Although a continuing part of camp activities, ideological work among inmates remained secondary to economic production in the Nikishov era. For the most part, only those propaganda goals that helped raise industrial output survived the close of the 1930s. As a result, Dalstroi bosses reinvoked Stakhanovism as a spur to labor productivity in the camps. Identified and rewarded at all enterprises

40. *Sovetskaia Kolyma*, December 26, 1940, 1.
41. Ibid.

of the state trust, individual Stakhanovites again became media darlings throughout the Nikishov era and a ready, if by then hackneyed, symbol of superior work effort. As in Berzin's time, these productive inmates received hero status and the perquisites and benefits intended to stimulate other inmates. In honor of the fifth anniversary of the Stakhanov campaign, Dalstroi glorified the inmates at the Upper At-Uriakh camp for meeting their annual mining quota by August 30, 1940. Among the rewards handed out to prisoners for this achievement was a rarefied honor typical of the age in Magadan. In line with his cultural pretensions, Nikishov sent a troupe from the Gorky Theater in town to perform for the victorious inmates.[42]

In contrast to his revival of incentive programs from the early to mid-1930s, Nikishov did not emphasize Berzin's ethereal goals of inmate rehabilitation. The lofty rhetoric of Dalstroi's earliest years, which included the concepts of "reforging" and "reeducation through labor," continued to fade in importance throughout the 1940s.[43] This reflected a political divide between the Old Bolsheviks, within whose ranks Berzin can be counted, and the generation of officialdom represented by Nikishov, who molded the sentiments of late Stalinism. Affected by the catastrophe of the Great Purges and Stalin's harshening political line, younger members of the party elite reflected the more cynical values that had shaped their careers. Although rarefied terminology on the possibility of prisoner rehabilitation remained in their political vocabulary, it did not resonate well with the NKVD worldview recrafted by Stalin and the Great Terror. Even if inmates were no longer to be eliminated or simply marginalized on a wide scale, camp administrators saw them as

42. Ibid., August 31, 1940, 1.
43. In such attitudes, both Nikishov and Pavlov stood directly opposed to the more utopian Berzin. See A. I. Shirokov and M. M. Etlis, *Sovetskii period istorii Severo-Vostoka Rossii* (Magadan: Mezhdunarodnyi pedagogicheskii institut, 1993), 8.

equivalent to material investments or other supplies and thus as tools for achieving state policy. Uninterested in the more humanitarian vision of the Berzin era, the new Dalstroi chief concentrated on economic mandates from the Kremlin. Earlier idealistic views served as mere turns of phrase for Nikishov and his assistants, all of whom were jaded functionaries sent to Magadan with the express purpose of reanimating Dalstroi as an industrial concern.

As a means of stimulating production, however, the new measures often did not work according to plan. The state trust was able to return to the output capability of before the Great Purges, but only in relative terms. The camps were an important part of industrial planning in the Stalin era, when various agencies became addicted to the possibilities of vast and cheap inmate contingents. But for a number of reasons, the inefficiency and incompetence of the workforce meant that the standards of forced labor remained low. Aside from the inveterate shortcomings of prison enterprises, the Gulag faced difficulties, rampant in Soviet society, which only compounded this situation. Dalstroi produced large quantities of gold and other minerals, but at lower rates of productivity, partly because of the inherent limiting factor of political repressions, such as the Terror in 1937 and 1938, which reduced economic efficiency in spasmodic waves. Although enshrining industrialization and modernization as long-term goals of the state, the Stalin government was never able to overcome the repressive political inclinations that consistently undermined its own economy.

Building Norilsk

Simon Ertz

NORILSK IS TODAY a city of some two hundred thousand residents located in the Krasnoiarsk Territory of Northern Siberia on the Taimyr Peninsula. It is the northernmost major city of Russia and the world's second largest city, after Murmansk, above the Arctic Circle. It is linked by rail to the Kara Sea, and its mineral products can be shipped by the Northern Sea route. In winter the temperature drops to minus 45 degrees Fahrenheit, and Norilsk is without sun for months at a time. The Norilsk region contains more than a third of the world's nickel reserves, and 40 percent of the world's reserves of platinum as well as significant amounts of cobalt and copper.[1] Between 1935 and 1953, Norilsk housed one-third of a million prisoners of the Soviet Gulag, who constructed its facilities and then mined and processed its minerals. This chapter describes the building of this remote and gigantic industrial complex by Gulag prisoners.

The Gulag economy can be studied through its history, its

1. http://econ.1a.psu.edu/~bickes/norilsk.htm.

administrative structure, or its economic functions.[2] Yet if we focus
on the working arrangements of the Gulag, we may learn more
about them by studying the parts of the Gulag than by studying the
whole. This chapter provides a case study of a Gulag camp and its
associated industrial complexes, located in Norilsk and its environs.
Chapter 5 described the Norilsk labor force. The current chapter
deals with the construction of the Norilsk metallurgical complex,
its transportation infrastructure, and the Norilsk Correctional-
Labor Camp, called Norillag (meaning Norilsk camp), which was
created in 1935 and operated until 1956. This chapter examines the
decision to build Norilsk, the subsequent decision to turn the project
over to the NKVD and its Gulag administration for development,
and finally, Norilsk's difficult construction starting in 1935. This
account is based on original Norilsk archival documents from the
Soviet state and party archives.

EXPLORATION AND DESIGN

The geological study of the Norilsk area began in earnest in the
early 1920s,[3] but the first large expedition, consisting of 250 experts,
was dispatched to Norilsk only in 1930. This expedition was under
the auspices of the Main Administration for Nonferrous Metal and
Gold of the Supreme Council of the National Economy, which took
on the initial responsibility for developing Norilsk's reserves. The
expedition concluded that the Norilsk deposits were rich enough to
warrant the start-up of development. In 1933 about 500 workers,
employees, engineers, and technicians were already working on this

2. M. Dzhekobson and M. B. Smirnov, "Sistema Mest Zakluchenia v RSFSR
i SSSR. 1917–1930," *Sistema Ispravitel'no-Trudovyh Lagerey v SSSR. Spravochnik* (Moscow, 1998), p. 10–24; M. B. Smirnov, S. P. Sigachaev, and D. V. Shkapov,
Sistema Mest Zakluchenia v SSSR. 1929–1960 (Ukaz. soch.) pp. 25–74; O. V.
Khlevnyuk, "Prinuditel'niy Trud v Ekonomike SSSR, 1929–1941," *Svobodnaia
Mysl'*, 1992. No. 13. pp. 73–84.
3. N. N. Urvantsev, *Otkrytie Norilska* (Moscow, 1981).

task at Norilsk, but their number was too small for significant progress.[4] The exploration and development of Norilsk remained largely under the heavy industry ministry until 1935, when it was transferred to the NKVD and its Gulag administration. This transfer was legalized by the top-secret Council of People's Commissars Decree No. 1275-198ss., dated June 23, 1935, "About Norilsk nickel industrial complex construction,"[5] which documented that the infrastructure surrendered to the NKVD was minimal.[6] Thus, the Gulag administration had to start the construction of Norilsk practically from zero.

The minerals of the Norilsk area were significant for Soviet industry. The most valuable mineral was nickel, contained in local ores, which also had significant traces of copper, cobalt, and precious metals, such as platinum. Although platinum, copper, and cobalt later acquired considerable significance, nickel was at the time considered the basic product to be produced in Norilsk. As today, nickel in the 1930s was mainly used in the production of high-quality stainless steel, which was sought after by the military. In 1935 when the decision was made to proceed with development, only a small part of the actual deposits was known. Two years later, estimates of recoverable reserves were raised by a factor of six. According to 1939 data, Norilsk's deposits of nickel made up "48 percent of all deposits in the USSR and 22 percent of world deposits, not including the USSR." Copper deposits equaled "10 percent of USSR deposits and 2 percent of world deposits."[7] According to an October 1938 report, platinum deposits " . . . appear to equal 549,780 tons, which puts them in first place in USSR and accords

4. *Sovetskiy Taymyr*. May 30, 1933. Quotation from: A. L. L'vov, Noril'sk. Krasnoyarsk, 1985, p. 28.

5. State Archive of Russian Federation (hereafter—GARF). 5446.1.481: 194–199.

6. Ibid. See also GARF 9414.1.854: 4–28. Ibid. 968: 1–46.

7. GARF 9414.1.29: 54.

them status of world significance."[8] Natural conditions were favorable for the mining and processing of Norilsk ores because large deposits of rich coal were located in the region and served as a power supply both for smelting and for the transportation facilities operated by the Northern Sea Route Administration, the Merchant Marine Ministry, and the Yenisei Steam Navigation Company.[9]

Thus, the enormous economic and military significance of Norilsk was well established at the start of the second half of the 1930s when responsibility for exploiting these riches was placed squarely on the shoulders of the Gulag. The Council of People's Commissars decree of June 23, 1935, assigned the NKVD the responsibility of constructing the Norilsk nickel complex and obliged the NKVD "to organize a special camp for this purpose."[10] The June 1935 decree made Norilsk a top-priority construction project and provided the basic specifications and terms of its realization. The complex should be designed to produce "10,000 tons of nickel annually," and its launch was scheduled for 1938, after three years of construction. The NKVD was obliged to "begin an open field operation of Norilsk deposits starting January 1, 1936," "to complete its exploratory and research work in 1935," and "to ensure the completion of the fifteen-kilometer narrow-gauge rail link between Norilsk and Piasino and the 120-kilometer rail link between Norilsk and Dudinka by the end of 1936." The project design was assigned to a special design group of the Ministry of Heavy Industry, which was to be formed from the best experts of Union-Nickel-Project-Design (Soiuznikel'proekt). The deadline for completing the design was set for August 1, 1936.[11] Norilsk's pri-

8. Russian State Archive of the Economy (hereafter—GAE) 9022.3.1694: 16.
9. GARF 9414.1.29: 53.
10. SNK Decree No. 1275-198ss. of June 23, 1935, GARF 5446.1.481: 195.
11. Ibid. For a history of this design group, see A. A. Mironov, "25 Let Nikelevoy i Kobal'tovoy Promyshlennosti Sovetskogo Souza i Perspektiva ee Razvitiia,"

ority can be seen in the way in which the Ministry of Heavy Industry supplied Norilsk fully and ahead of schedule with experts, scientific and technical consultations, and studies of "correct management of construction operations."[12] The financing for the design and purchase of equipment and materials was to come directly from the Council of People's Commissars' own reserve funds. Ten million rubles were assigned to Norilsk in 1935 alone. The State Planning Commission was authorized to allocate additional funds for equipment and materials within ten days to take advantage of the short navigation period in summertime.

The decision to assign Norilsk to the Gulag administration of the NKVD was made gradually. The original intent was to assign construction and operation to civilian ministries while the Gulag supplied prison labor force. The Politburo issued its most important decisions as joint decrees with the Council of People's Commissars. According to this practice, the July 1932 joint decree of the Central Committee and the Council of People's Commissars, "About Norilsk deposits of platinum and other rare metals," was introduced and accepted at the July 10, 1932, meeting of the Politburo. Paragraph 8 called on the OGPU (the predecessor of the NKVD) to "ensure exploratory work with the required labor force." Since the OGPU managed only penal labor, it is clear that the Politburo had already decided in 1932, just as the White Sea–Baltic Canal was being completed, that Norilsk would be built by Gulag inmates. The first group of prisoners arrived in Norilsk three years later. The 1932 joint decree assigned Norilsk projects to different authorities. The surveying for railway construction between Norilsk and the Yenisei River was assigned to the Ministry of Transport; equipment and expert geologists were assigned to the Ministry of Heavy Indus-

Nauchno-Tekhnicheskoe Obschestvo Tsvetnoy Metallurgii: Dvadtsat' Piat' Let Nikelevoy Promyshlennosti SSSR (Moscow, 1959), pp. 5–14.

12. SNK Decree No. 1275-198ss. of June 23, 1935, GARF 5446.1.481: 195.

try and the Committee for Labor and Defense; radio communications were assigned to the communications ministry; and geological exploration was assigned to "Eastern Gold" (Vostokzoloto). Geological exploration was supervised by the Main Administration for Nonferrous Metals and Gold (Glavtsvetmetzoloto). The OGPU was responsible only for the delivery of labor force.[13]

The leadership's conception of Norilsk changed in 1935, when Norilsk was assigned exclusively to the Gulag administration of the NKVD. The 1935 about-face is explained by the Gulag's growing reputation for managing large projects in remote regions and difficult conditions and by the civilian ministries' aversion to working under such hazardous conditions. The development of Norilsk deposits was extremely difficult because of its remote location beyond the Artic Circle. The Ministry of Heavy Industry, which was responsible for metallurgy, for all practical purposes refused to take on the Norilsk project. In fact, the heavy industry ministry lobbied to be relieved of responsibility for such a difficult project. The People's Commissar of Heavy Industry, G. K. Ordzhonikidze, wrote to Stalin the following: "Taking into account serious difficulties in the realization of exploratory and research operations, completion of construction and the development of production in polar conditions, and also the enormous experience of the OGPU in carrying out complex construction projects in extremely difficult conditions, we conclude it is expedient to entrust the OGPU with the organization of operations on the basis of a special camp."[14]

Geologist A. E. Vorontsov supervised the exploration of Norilsk deposits from the beginning of the 1930s, and in 1935 he was

13. Russian State Archive of Social and Political History (hereafter—RGASPI) 17.3.891: 41–42.
14. L. P. Rasskazov, I. V. Uporov, *Ispol'zovanie i Pravovoe Regulirovanie Truda Osuzhdennyh v Rossiyskoy Istorii* (Krasnodar, 1998), pp. 61–62—quotation from Ordzhonikidze's letter is taken from S. I. Kuz'min, "Ot GUMZA do GUINa," *Prestuplenie i Nakazanie*, 1997, No. 5, p. 11.

appointed the first chief engineer of "Norilsk-construction" (Norils-troi). In the spring of that year, he was present at a Politburo meeting in which the draft of the 1935 decree was discussed. Vorontsov gave the following brief account of the discussion: "Stalin recommended that the project be transferred not to Otto Ul'evich Shmidt [then the chief of the Administration for the Northern Sea Route]; he has enough to worry about. It should go to the construction organizations of the NKVD."[15] Although it was unusual for the Politburo to discuss basic decisions in the presence of outsiders, the reason for the decision to transfer responsibility for Norilsk to the NKVD was obvious. The Gulag administration had evolved in the minds of top Soviet leaders from an organization that supplied prison labor to an administration that could, on its own, carry out complex construction projects of the highest priority. As noted in Chapters 3, 8, and 9, the Gulag's potential had become apparent with the construction of the White Sea–Baltic Canal, the beginning of construction on the Baikal-Amur Railroad (BAM) in 1932, and the organization of camps formed to carry out other significant economic projects.[16] Hence, the assignment of the Norilsk complex to the Gulag administration in 1935 was yet another step in this logical progression.

ORGANIZING THE NORILSK PROJECT

Only two days after the approval of the Council of People's Commissars decree, the NKVD Commissar, G. G. Yagoda, signed top-secret order No. 00239 of June 25, 1935, "About the organization of Norilsk Nickel Complex construction."[17] The camp was named

15. V. N. Lebedinskiy, P. I. Mel'nikov, Ukaz. soch., pp. 13–14. See also A. L. L'vov, Ukaz. soch., pp. 28–29.

16. M. B. Smirnov, S. P. Sigachaev, D.V. Shkapov, Ukaz. soch., pp. 30–33.

17. A. I. Kokurin, N. V. Petrov, *GULAG: Struktura i Kadry* (Svobodnaia Mysl', 2000, No. 2), p. 113.

"Norilsk Correctional Labor Camp" (acronym Norilsk ITL) and was generally referred to as "Norillag." Yagoda's order assigned to the NKVD's Gulag administration more complex and detailed tasks than the Council of People's Commissars decree upon which it was based: Yagoda called for the permanent exploitation of mineral deposits and for the development of the whole area in accord with the now-customary practice of assigning large-scale projects in remote northern and eastern regions to the Gulag. The Gulag's labor camps were to provide labor and other services to the associated industrial projects, such as the Norilsk Construction (Norilstroi) and then to the mineral and metallurgical plants to be built.[18] A precursor of the Norilsk complex, the Northeastern Labor Camp, was organized in April 1932 to provide labor for the "Dalstroi" trust (see Chapter 6).[19] The amount of detail in Yagoda's order underscores the significance of Norilsk in comparison with other large Gulag projects. Norilsk had strategic importance, and its difficult geographical conditions made the project a technologically difficult and complex undertaking. Norilsk had long winters and violent snowstorms and was remote from all means of transport. Construction, which was carried out under conditions of permafrost, required new construction technologies. The difficult climate is mentioned directly in the ninth article of Yagoda's order: "Considering the importance of Norilsk and its location in extremely difficult conditions, I impose as a duty on all bodies of the NKVD to respond immediately to all inquiries of Gulag or Norilsk camp concerning this construction."[20] Another indication of Norilsk's importance is that Yagoda directly assigned Norilsk to the Gulag

18. M. Dzhekobson, M. B. Smirnov, Ukaz. soch., pp. 18–19; M. B. Smirnov, S. P. Sigachaev, D. V. Shkapov, Ukaz. soch., pp. 25–26.

19. *Sistema Ispravitel'no-Trudovykh Lagerey v SSSR. Spravochnik*, pp. 382–385.

20. NKVD top-secret order No. 00239 of June 25, 1935: A. I. Kokurin, N. V. Petrov, Ukaz. soch., p. 114.

administration. In May of 1935—one month before the order to organize the Norilsk camp—most camp administrations were subordinate to territorial NKVD administrations. Only five camps "occupied with construction of major economic projects," were directly subordinate to the Gulag administration.[21] Norilsk was added as the sixth by order of Yagoda.

During the first three years of the project, Norilsk development was based on two entities—the Norilsk camp (Norillag) and Norilsk construction (Norilstroi). The second was the agency in charge of building Norilsk's infrastructure using penal labor from Norillag. The director of Norilstroi was initially in charge of the overall project. The draft plan of 1935 called for a production capacity of ten thousand tons of nickel a year starting in 1938, a figure that was first achieved (approximately) only in 1945. As it became clear that start-up schedules could not be met, amendments to the original plan were made. A Council of People's Commissars decree of April 26, 1938, proposed to start exploitation of the first production line (with a productive capacity of five thousand tons a year) in 1940 and to complete construction in 1941.[22] Documents from 1939 and 1940 did not project dates for when the complex would reach its proposed productive capacity and targeted only insignificant quantities of nickel production for the near future.[23] Soviet accounts of the Norilsk project remained silent on the significant delays; instead, Norilsk was described as entering production after a period of speedy construction.[24]

21. These camps were the Baikal-Amur, White Sea–Baltic Canal, Dmitrovsky, Uhta-Pechora and Temnikovsky camps. M. B. Smirnov, S. P. Sigachaev, D. V. Shkapov, Ukaz. soch., p. 39.

22. This decree was published in *Ekonomika Gulaga i ee Rol' v Razvitii Strany, 30-e gody* (Sbornik dokumentov, RAN. Institut Rossiyskoy Istorii, sost. M.I. Khlusov, Moscow, 1998), pp. 88–89.

23. GARF 9414.1.2977: 231b. Ibid. 29: 57. Ibid. 30: 43.

24. E. Riabchikov, *Plamia nad Arktikoy* (Moscow, 1959); V. A. Dar'ial'skiy, *Noril'sku—25 let* (Noril'sk, 1960); V. N. Lebedinskiy, P. I. Mel'nikov, Ukaz.

Norilsk construction suffered from significant cost overruns. The draft plan of 1938 called for a capital expenditure of 515 million rubles. This cost estimate was raised to 1.1 billion rubles in 1939 and 1940 and was later set at 1.3 billion rubles. These cost overruns were partly related to the difficult climate and to transport difficulties, but they also reflected fundamental changes in the nature of the project. As geologists discovered ever-richer mineral deposits in the region, the design focus changed from a complex that would produce semifabricated metals to one that would finish metals. As geologists found unusually rich lodes with high nickel contents, the decision was made in 1939 to expand the Norilsk plant from an experimental plant to a significant industrial complex.[25] According to the original plans of 1935, Norilsk's major product was to be semiprocessed nickel, rather than anodic or electrolytic (cathode) nickel, which was supposed to be processed in Krasnoyarsk.[26] Yet the 1939 decision meant that facilities for the final part of the production process were to be installed at Norilsk. Correspondingly, by 1940 the capability of the complex was defined not in terms of semifinished material but by "10 tons of nickel and 17 tons of copper annually." The increase in the construction budget (noted above, from 515 million to 1.1 billion rubles) was due in

---

Soch.; V. N. Lebedinskiy, *V Serdtse Rudnogo Pritaymyr'ia*; V. N. Lebedinskiy, "Nikel' dlia Fronta," *Voprosy Istorii*, 1981 No. 5, pp. 181–185; B. I. Kolesnikov, *Forpost Industrii v Sibirskom Zapoliar'ie. 50 let Noril'skomu Gornomo-Metallurgicheskomu Kombinatu im. A. P. Zaveriagina* (Krasnoyarsk, 1985); A. L. L'vov, Ukaz. soch. For a short account of the plant's history see also M. Ya. Vazhnov, *Bol'shoy Noril'sk: Istoria Sotsial'no-Ekonomicheskogo Razvitia. 1960–1985* (Otechestvennaia Istoria, 1994, No. 6), pp. 74–75.

25. Yu. L. Edel'khanov, "Sovershenstvovanie Tekhnologii Proizvodstva Noril'skogo Gorno-Metallurgicheskogo Kombinata," Dvadtsat' Piat' Let Nikelevoy Promyshlennosti SSSR. Materialy nauchno-tekhnicheskogo soveschania, posviaschennogo 25-letiu nikelevoy promyshlennosti SSSR, August 4–5, 1958, Verkhniy Ufaley (Moscow, 1959), p. 74.

26. SNK Decree No. 1275-198ss. of June 23, 1935.

part to the change to final processing.[27] It is difficult to disentangle the cost overruns due to such fundamental design changes from those associated with normal construction difficulties. Nevertheless, we will examine endogenous reasons for cost overruns in the next section.

FAILURES, EXCUSES, AND PROGRESS

Norilstroi, the Gulag organization in charge of building Norilsk's infrastructure, had to fulfill plans imposed on it by the Council of People's Commissars and by the commissar of the NKVD. Like any other Soviet organization responsible for fulfilling plans, Norilstroi wished to present its work to its superiors in the most favorable light. Its failures had to be explained as caused by the failures of others or by forces outside of management's control. Until 1941, Norilsk's reports were sent to the Gulag administration for review by the NKVD; thereafter they were sent to a new central administrative board within the Gulag, the Central Administration of Mining Enterprise Camps.[28] Norilsk's reports included not only statistical results but also narratives describing the course of construction and special problems and difficulties encountered. The Norilsk administration used these reports to justify their claims on resources and to ensure that their superiors understood the difficult conditions under which they were operating. Norilsk was so remote that it was difficult for Moscow to check the reports, giving Norilsk a certain leeway to fudge them.

Reports from the first three years, beginning in 1935, when the first group of more than one thousand prisoners arrived in midyear, show the extreme difficulty and hardship associated with creating new infrastructure in such a hostile environment. During this

27. GARF 9414.1.30: 41.
28. *Sistema Ispravitel'no-Trudovykh Lagerey v SSSR*, pp. 108–109.

period, the mining of coal and ores began, but construction activities concentrated "almost exclusively on construction of subsidiary facilities,"[29] such as transportation systems. For this reason, reports from the scene are less detailed than in later periods.[30] The first three years coincide with Norilsk's first management team, led by Vladimir Matveev. It fell to Matveev to explain to Gulag authorities a series of plan "failures"; the 1936 report had to explain why the plan of capital construction had not been executed. Although 33 million rubles of investment had been planned (in constant plan prices), actual investment was only 78 percent of that planned. The physical construction plan was fulfilled by only 51 percent, and construction costs were 9 percent higher than scheduled. Despite shortfalls in construction results, expenditures on construction materials exceeded the planned amount by 21 percent.[31] The 1936 report also explained why some important projects were not started (such as an experimental concentrating mill and a second temporary power station).

The management explained some plan "deviations" by citing decisions to redirect resources because of unusual circumstances, such as "the necessity to promptly launch temporary railroad traffic." Other narratives explained deviations that were outside of management's control.[32] The delay of a forty-ship expedition loaded with materials and equipment was particularly catastrophic:[33] " . . . From the 22,700 tons of consignments expected, only 6,000 tons reached the settlement nearest to Norilsk; 1,700 tons were sent

29. GARF 9414.1.29: 55.
30. T. Vensenostseva, *Sozdanie Opornoy Bazy dlia Stroitel'stva NGMK. Noril'lag pri V.Z. Matveeve* (Noril'skiy Memorial, vypusk October 4, 1998), pp. 23–25.
31. GARF 9414.1.854: 73–76, 93.
32. Ibid., 74.
33. RGASPI 17.3.975: 16; G. Kublitskiy, "Khodili my na Piasinu . . .," *Sibirskie Ogni*. 1968, No.12, pp. 127–139.

back; and 15,000 tons were kept on Lake Piasino for the winter."[34] Not only was the delivery of building materials and equipment incomplete, but because of the congestion at the port of Dudinka, the overexpenditures on labor for loading and unloading cargo were significant. The 1936 report complained that the slow delivery of prisoners due to "supply and transport difficulties"[35] caused the loss of four hundred thousand man-days "during the best construction season."[36] The 1936 report also complained about the bad physical and "moral" state of arriving prisoners, about cost limits that were unrealistic for Arctic conditions, and about "conducting work without preliminary drafts and without effective management."[37]

The minutes of the industrial managers' meeting of Norilstroi and Norillag were added to the 1936 report as an extraordinary communication to superiors to summarize the immense difficulties under which Norilsk was operating:

> It should be noted that materials of the annual report and its narrative reflect insufficiently the circumstances of construction work under absolutely abnormal conditions: . . . In 1935 an advance group of workers was sent to undeveloped tundra without necessary materials to prepare for expanding construction in 1936. This contingent had to do difficult and time-consuming preparatory work under permafrost conditions, under the most severe snowstorms, which dissipated their energy and mental state. Only a person who had experienced it himself knows what it means to preserve the necessary vitality and working energy after months of constant winds with a force from 18 up to 37 meters per second that blow continuous clouds of snow, so that visibility is about 2 meters. Stray workers were lost due to loss of orientation. They had to work in temperatures reaching 53 degrees below zero. Workers were dispersed in the tundra to pre-

34. GARF 9414.1.854: 9.
35. GARF 9414.1.854: 2b.
36. GARF 9414.1.854: 74.
37. GARF 9414.1.854: 2b.

pare new areas for habitation and to prepare the area to receive new labor force, create stocks of materials, and to equip work places. In these conditions, Norilstroi workers conducted the first operations in making tractor and cart roads from Dudinka to Norilsk. . . .[38]

The winter of 1936 was the first Arctic experience of Norilsk's first general manager, Matveev, who had grown up in Central Asia.[39] It was Matveev who included these graphic pictures of Norilsk working conditions for his superiors in the Gulag administration. The descriptions were designed to drive home the point that norms and plans drawn up in Moscow were unrealistic when applied to Arctic construction. Norilsk's superiors, however, did not accept Matveev's "excuses" at face value. "The commentary to the report of Norilstroi," signed jointly by the Gulag's chief of the mining sector and by the deputy head of the finance-planning sector, complains of "inept maneuvering of the labor force" [underlined in red pencil] and of significant overexpenditure of funds, where the "available data do not clarify reasons for the large gap between the supply plan and its fulfillment."[40] Despite Matveev's attempt to explain to the Gulag administration why the work was over budget and behind schedule, these comments show that the Gulag administration considered Norilsk as a construction project that, although complex, should be finished on time and with the allocated resources. Although they recognized that emergency situations influenced the 1936 results, they supposed that subsequent work could be completed according to schedule. The Gulag administration brushed off Matveev's doubts—that Norilsk could be finished according to plan—by offering increased mechanization, improvements in the qualifications of prisoners and workers, and the estab-

38. GARF 9414.1.854: 2–3.
39. V. N. Lebedinskiy, P. I. Melnikov, Ukaz. soch., p. 22.
40. GARF 9414.1.854: 74, 76.

lishment of more strict control over Norilstroi by the Gulag administration.[41]

We have even richer documentation for the economic activities of 1937 because this year produced two reports, one by the soon-to-be-fired management team of Matveev, and the second by the incoming administration led by A. P. Zaveniagin.[42] Matveev's report contains a litany of plan failures: "1937 was supposed to be the year of completion of preparatory work. In 1937 it was necessary, first of all, to solve the issue of the main supply base located on the coast of the Yenisei River in Dudinka village" by completing a narrow-gauge railway line connecting Dudinka and Norilsk. Matveev reports that "this basic task of 1937 was not completed; the railway was opened only at the end of October in a condition unsuitable for exploitation in the severe climatic conditions of the Arctic Circle."[43] As a result, "the whole construction plan was foiled." The secondary power station and the experimental-enrichment factory "were not only incomplete; they were still in a rudimentary state at the end of the year."[44] These important failures are reflected in the lag of construction behind schedule: only 40 percent of scheduled investment was carried out,[45] although 212 percent of the scheduled costs were expended. The totals for 1937 were disastrous from the point of view of central economic administrators. Yet nothing suggests that the 1937 annual plan was changed when it became clear that its execution was impossible. As in 1936, Matveev continued to blame the plan failure on insufficient construction materials: "In the first half-year and in the third quarter there was no extensive construction in Norilsk, a fact explained by the lack

41. GARF 9414.1.854: 83.
42. GARF 9414.1.968: 1–46; GARF 9414.1.969: 2–17.
43. V. A. Dar'ial'skiy, Ukaz. soch., p. 16; RGAE 8704.1.948: 14.
44. GARF 9414.1.968: 2, 4–5.
45. GARF 9414.1.968: 14; GARF 9414.1.969: 4-6; GARF 8361.1.10: 19.

of construction materials."[46] The missing construction materials were then explained by the failure of the 1936 supply mission and by problems in railway construction. Matveev had the temerity to place some of the blame for supply problems on Moscow: "All major supply questions are resolved in Moscow, but Norilsk is remote from Moscow and the frequently severe conditions of Norilstroi are not taken into account," such as the difficulty of navigating the Yenisei River and the "carelessness and mismatch of the scheduled and estimated norms that regulate the operations of Norilstroi."[47] Matveev also complained about the application of "single all-union norms to Arctic Circle conditions," which had to be applied because there were no others. "Such high norms mean the underestimation of budget rates of work."[48]

The Gulag administration's reaction to Matveev's tales of failure is found in the protocol of a 1937 meeting of the Gulag balance commission chaired by the Gulag chief, I. I. Pliner. The Gulag administration's assessment of Norilsk management was merciless:

> The improper use of labor has caused a failure to fulfill the plan of construction of the narrow-gauge railroad from Dudinka to Norilsk. . . . Not only was the directive on cost reduction not executed, but a large over-expenditure over the cost estimate was allowed. . . . In view of the massive failure to fulfill the construction plan and the vast over-expenditures, we declare the industrial and economic activity of Norilsk construction to be completely unsatisfactory and uneconomical.[49]

In light of its disastrous assessment of Matveev's performance, it comes as no surprise that the Gulag protocol mentions the appointment of a new general manager for Norilsk, A. P. Zavenia-

46. GARF 9414.1.968: 19.
47. GARF 9414.1.968: 2–3.
48. GARF 9414.1.968: 45.
49. GARF 9414.1.969: 108.

gin, who took over Norilsk operations in early April 1938.[50] The reasons for Matveev's firing are related in the classified NKVD Order No. 044, "About operation of NKVD Norillag," which was approved literally on the eve of these events, March 9, 1938. It cites the massive failure of the 1937 construction plan due to "poor organization of work," the "absence of work discipline," and "cronyism" and "drunkenness" among the camp management. The management of the Gulag was ordered to develop a plan to complete the railroad construction before the end of 1938, to introduce a system of monthly operation schedules and strictly monitor their fulfillment, to finance Norilsk on the basis of work accomplished to prevent cost overruns, and to strengthen its management and engineering staff. Ominously (since this report was issued during the Great Purges), the Gulag administration issued a "stern reprimand" to Matveev and warned him "that in case of non-fulfillment of the plan for the first six months of 1938 he will be prosecuted." These warnings appeared too late. Matveev, the first general director of Norilsk, was arrested one month later.[51] On April 9, 1939, the military tribunal of the Moscow NKVD sentenced him to death, a sentence later commuted to a fifteen-year prison term.[52] In 1955 he was rehabilitated post mortem.

The new general manager, Zaveniagin, in his first report concerning the 1937 Norilsk performance, places the blame on his predecessor. After an exposition of the huge cost overruns, Zaveniagin concludes that "the 1937 over-expenditure was not justified

50. Zaveniagin was appointed chief of Norilstroi by order No. 840ls NKVD SSSR of April 8, 1938 (A. I. Kokurin, N. V. Petrov, "Gulag: Struktura i Kadry." Statia Sed'maia. *Svobodnaia Mysl'*. 2000, No. 3, p. 106). His assignment was approved during the Politburo meeting of April 25, 1938 (RGASPI 17.3.998:15).

51. *Sistema Ispravitel'no-Trudovykh Lagerey v SSSR*, p. 339.

52. A. I. Kokurin, N. V. Petrov, Uraz. Soch., *Svobodnaia Mysl'*, 2000, No. 3, pp. 107–117; Pritcha o Noril'ske. B.m., b.g. p. 7. (Post-Soviet publication of the Museum of Development and Evolution of Norilsk Industrial Complex).

by any external factors." The report criticizes the extremely low labor productivity of separate construction projects, including railway construction, "the absence of means of mechanization in the construction place, the performance of labor-intensive operations in wintertime, and insufficiently qualified workforce. . . ." As for the problem of the delivery of materials to Norilsk, the report concludes that despite the "poor organization of the shipments from Krasnoyarsk to Dudinka," "the quantity of deliveries to Dudinka during the navigation period of 1937 was sufficient for fulfillment of the capital construction plan. The solution of the supply question required only the prompt delivery of materials by railroad to Norilsk."[53]

The new management began its work with a significant reorganization of both the camp and the construction organization. The camp, Norillag, which "included the camp divisions and the department of general supplies and its commercial network," was separated from Norilstroi, the construction company, and was placed on an independent accounting system. Several new departments were formed, including a budget department with a staff of up to two hundred people, a department of work organization, an operations department, a department of design, a maintenance subdivision, a subdivision of subcontracting enterprises, and a chief mechanic's department. This reorganization was supposed to "define precisely the obligations and responsibilities of each division." The functioning of the management of construction before this reorganization was criticized as follows: "Before the second quarter there were so-called 'areas,' which merged production and camp functions."[54]

The 1938 report of the new management team spelled out its assessment of the situation and its accomplishments since the new

53. GARF 9414.1.969: 6, 8, 10.
54. GARF 9414.1.1118: 6, 9.

management team took over: "January to May was a period of complete stagnation of construction due to the lack of materials that remained in Dudinka and could not be dispatched owing to unavailability of railway transportation. From June to the second half of August, forces were concentrated on the completion of the railway to make it operative. September through December saw a period of normal turnover of goods from Dudinka and full-scale operations in Norilsk."[55] Zaveniagin's statistical results also showed marked improvement. Capital investments composed 52 million rubles or 104 percent of the authorized investment plan without, remarkably, cost overruns. Originally a higher 60-million-ruble investment plan had been authorized, but it was cut back to 50 million in October.[56] However, the level of 1938 investment was approximately twice as high as in the previous year. Norilsk's ability to carry out construction work blossomed after the start-up of normal railway transportation.

Figure 7.1 shows planned and realized investments in Norilsk for the period 1935–39. These data show that the crisis period for Norilsk construction was 1937, when Norilsk's managers and prison workers had to contend with the rigors of work in Arctic conditions and with the plan failures that were bound to occur, such as the failure of the forty-ship convoy in 1936. Once Norilsk's transportation infrastructure and reasonably reliable lines of supply were established, construction could proceed on a more normal basis. Matveev had the bad luck to be manager during this difficult period. Later management teams could build off the "failures" of his tenure. Significant construction problems remained. Although the 1938 construction plan had been fulfilled in investment expenditures, results with respect to putting finished projects into operation were less satisfactory. The completion of several major projects,

55. Ibid.
56. GARF 9414.1.1118: 5, 9.

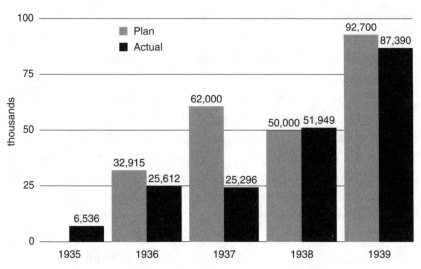

Figure 7.1   The Dynamics of Capital Investments at Norilsk Construction (in Thousand Rubles)
Sources: GARF 9414.1.854: 73; 969: 4; 1118: 16; 1.2977: 230ob.; 8361.1.102: 4.

such as the temporary Power Plant Number 2 and a few construction-materials plants scheduled for operation in 1938, were postponed until 1939, though many of them were almost finished. The delays in putting these plants into operation were caused by defects of planning, analyzed in detail in the explanatory notes to the 1938 report. For example, many of Union-Nickel-Design's plans were not suitable to Arctic conditions and had to be redesigned at the site. Supply problems continued to be severe, particularly the shortage of lumber.[57] The start-up delays, however, were also explained by frequent design changes brought about by changing circumstances. The mining of rich ores that could be smelted without enrichment required the redesign of several factories under construction. Moreover, there was no construction-financial plan, which "deprived management of the possibilities of monitoring and

57. GARF 9414.1.1118: 6, 10, 12.

controlling budget discipline."[58] Even if there had been a better financial plan, it may have been beyond the capabilities of the camp's accounting departments, which "[had] only a tiny share of qualified workers; the majority of the accounting departments [were] staffed by barely literate people."[59] The optimal use of labor was another problem. The timing of the beginning of large projects was determined by the availability of large numbers of prisoners in the middle of the year. There were too few prisoner laborers in the third and fourth quarters.[60] What's more, Norilsk prisoners were ill suited for construction; they were primarily unskilled workers whose training was conducted on the work site, thereby reducing efficiency and quality of work.

Memoirs of former Norilsk prisoners shed light on the use of prison labor.[61] Although accounts differ, former penal workers all agree on the hard and cruel working conditions in Norilsk. Some, however, recall their work with pride, citing honorary postings on the "red bulletin board" for outstanding brigade work. Those who engaged in physical labor emphasize the labor intensity of their work. Prisoners who had to level construction sites or to dig excavations in permafrost worked only with pickaxes. Workers transporting construction materials or moving earth worked with primitive wooden wheelbarrows. They had to develop their own primitive technology for working in permafrost, such as a heating machine cobbled together by a political prisoner. Prisoners were assigned to work without consideration for their physical state or qualifications. Some of the weakest and oldest prisoners were assigned to the hardest form of manual labor, while the accounting

58. GARF 9414.1.1118: 7.
59. GARF 9414.1.1118: 20.
60. GARF 9414.1.1118: 10.
61. Memoirs of former prisoners can be found in the Archive of the Moscow Society of "Memorial" as well as on the website of the Krasnoyarsk Society of "Memorial" (http://memorial.krsk.ru/memuar).

department employed able-bodied but scarcely literate personnel.
Women assigned to conveyer belts that sorted ores in winter had to
jump up and down on the belts until they started up again. Prisoners
characterized their work as "hard, unproductive, and at times senseless." Some of them report being assigned street-cleaning duties on
national holidays, after being told by their guards: "National holidays are not for enemies of the people." Thus the prisoners themselves echo the complaints of their captors, who pleaded with the
Gulag administration for better equipment and technology. The
NKVD and its Gulag administration continued to assign the same
output norms to Norilsk prisoners, working under coercion and
with primitive hand tools, as to the civilian work force. For the
leadership, this prison labor was "free" and available in abundant
quantities. There would be no great loss if it were wasted or not
used to its full potential. Camp administrators viewed labor differ-
ently because plan fulfillment depended mainly on how effectively
labor was used and how motivated prison laborers were. If they did
not fulfill their plans, their managers would be demoted or, worse,
imprisoned, as the first general director of Norilsk had been.

SURPLUSES AND EXPECTATIONS

The first period of Norilsk construction and economic activity came
to an end in 1938 as Norilsk's second management team took
control. The chief transportation links had been established.
Norilsk mining operations were substantial. Norilsk produced
5,050 tons of ore in 1939; 30,130 tons in 1940; and 81,099 tons in
1941, of which 2,270 tons were high-grade ore. Norilsk was producing 4,000 tons of refined nickel by 1943. The Council of People's
Commissars' original production goal of producing 10,000 tons of
nickel by 1938 was met in 1945 as Soviet troops were placing the
Red Flag atop the Reichstag in Berlin. The war years were a difficult
period for Norilsk because of the increased demand for nickel and

the diversion of resources and workforce to the front. Throughout the period, the Gulag administration continued to receive complaints from Norilsk about the lack of labor and of scarcities in supplies. However, these complaints were not as vocal as in early years.

CONCLUSIONS

The story told here, based on the Gulag's own archives, is of how the Gulag administration took on a large priority infrastructure project that civilian ministries would not touch because of its risks. Civilian ministries, such as the heavy industry ministry, pleaded for the transfer of Norilsk to the Gulag administration with its masses of prisoner laborers that could be dispatched without complaint to the remotest and most arduous locations in the Soviet Union. After a difficult start, beginning at zero, prisoners were placed in a remote Arctic climate to build the housing and transportation infrastructure for what would become the Norilsk metallurgical complex. In this chapter the story has been told largely from a bureaucratic perspective. We have related how the NKVD willingly accepted the 1935 order to build Norilsk on its own and how the minister of interior imposed tough deadlines and tasks on the Gulag administration to complete the work on time. The NKVD refused to accept excuses for plan failure, even though plan failure seemed inevitable given the circumstances under which Norilstroi was operating. The first general manager was sacrificed, and the second management team arrived in time to take advantage of the enormous sacrifices that had taken place during the first three years of construction.

The ministry of heavy industry's near refusal to build Norilsk could be taken as a sign that it could have been built only by the Gulag—but this supposition would not be true. The heavy industry ministry simply recognized the difficulty and cost of the project and understood that the chance of failure was high. They followed the best course in opting out, particularly when the Gulag administration appeared ready to take over the project. The Gulag's own willingness is probably explained by their unrealistic expectation that prison labor could solve all problems.

The Norilsk reports show the clash between the reality of construction in the Arctic Circle (as viewed firsthand by Norilsk managers) and the expectations of the NKVD and its Gulag administration. The NKVD assumed that prison workers could be forced to be as productive as free labor working with better equipment and in better climates. Some of these coercive measures, such as more workdays and longer workhours, are summarized in Chapter 5. Norilsk administrators pleaded with Moscow for lower work norms to reflect the lack of equipment, the poor provisions, and the Arctic cold. Moscow insisted that Norilsk fulfill the plan and not resort to excuses. This clash between reality and expectation is visible in the enormous cost overruns of the early years. Costs were calculated based on unrealistic work norms; as worker performance fell well below norms, costs soared above those planned. In effect, the NKVD's plan was to extract a surplus from Norilsk workers by forcing them to work as effectively as civilian workers in more favorable locations. The massive failure of 1937 showed the lack of realism of this plan.

The White Sea–Baltic Canal

Mikhail Morukov

MAY 2003 MARKED the seventieth anniversary of the opening of the White Sea–Baltic Canal, the first waterway built by prisoner labor. Since its design phase, views on its expediency and its economic rationality have differed dramatically. Official Soviet publications of the 1930s, particularly articles by K. Lepin and I. S. Isakov and the "History of the Construction of the White Sea–Baltic Canal," published in the *History of Factories and Plants* and edited by Maksim Gorky, proclaimed the canal a success—even though Gorky's book was later banned in 1937. Starting in the 1980s, the activity of the Gulag in Karelia and its construction of the White Sea–Baltic Canal were subject to harsh criticism, for example, in Solzhenitsyn's *The Gulag Archipelago*. More recent publications give negative assessments of the canal.[1] This chapter

---

1. For a list of publications, see K. Lepin, *Belomorsko-Baltiyskiy Vodniy Put' i Rekonstrukzia Mariinskoy Sistemy* (Vodniy Transport, 1932, No. 7); I. S. Isakov, *Belomorsko-Baltiyskaya Magistral', Morskoy Sbornik*, 1932, No. 11–12); M. Gorkiy, L. Averbah, S. Firin (ed.), *Belomorsko-Baltiyskiy Kanal Imeni I. V. Stalina* (Moscow, 1934); *Istoria Otkrytiia i Osvoeniia Severnogo Morskogo Puti* (t. Sh-1U L. 1959–1969); *GULAG v Karelii 1930–1941, Sbornik Dokumentov*, (Petrozavodsk, 1992); G. M. Ivanova, *GULAG v Sisteme Totalitarnogo Gosudarstva*

uses Gulag archives to study the construction of the White Sea–
Baltic Canal, using the same documents that its builders used some
seventy years earlier. Chapters 3 and 6 mention the pivotal role of
the White Sea–Baltic Canal in the history of the Gulag. The canal
served as a testing ground for the use of forced labor in a massive
infrastructure project. The canal's speedy completion provided an
impetus for other similar projects, such as Dalstroi and the Moskva-
Volga Canal.

BACKGROUND

The notion of a canal that would connect the Baltic and White Seas
through the eastern territories of Karelia dates back to Peter the
Great, who three hundred years ago made the first transfer of sea
crafts from the White Sea to the Baltic Sea. The idea of a canal was
promoted over the next two hundred years, mainly by local authorities. For example, promoters in the Onega Lake region developed
two canal-construction projects, and a military expedition of 1798
and 1799 conducted a preliminary investigation in eastern Karelia
but concluded that such a canal was not feasible. Nevertheless, canal
designs continued to be drafted and discussed in 1824, 1835, 1855,
1867–75, 1889, and 1894 but failed to move forward. In each
instance, construction costs were too high for private financing, and
state financing was not available. From 1895 to 1909, the focus on
a northern connection was shifted to railway construction from
Vologda to Arkhangelsk. In 1909 the canal notion was revived
without consequence by the Russian Technical Society, and after
the start of World War I, the notion was raised three times in the

---

(Moscow, 1997); Yu. L. Diakov, *Razvitie Transportno-Dorozhnoy Seti SSSR v
1941–1945 gg.* (Moscow, 1997).

Naval Ministry but was never carried beyond preliminary investigation.[2]

Soon after the October Revolution of 1917, discussions of the White Sea–Baltic Canal project resurfaced. In the spring of 1918, the Supreme Economic Council of the Northern Region drafted a regional transportation plan, which included a White Sea to Ob railroad line and an Onega to White Sea canal. According to the plan, the railroad and canal would become the main axis of the northern transportation system, provide the base for developing the Ukhta-Pechersk oil region and the Kola mining region, and connect the northwestern industrial region with Siberia. In March of 1918, the University of Perm and the Supreme Economic Council prepared to dispatch research groups to these regions, but these plans were interrupted by the civil war.[3]

It was not until the spring of 1930 that the executive branch of the Soviet government, the Council of Labor and Defense, issued a report titled "Construction of the White Sea–Baltic Canal," which provided an economic and a military justification for the canal. The report proposed a canal of 18 feet (5.5 meters) depth. A canal of this depth, it was argued, would allow the transfer of navy ships and equipment from the Baltic Sea to the northern seas and would offer the economic advantage of the shipment of goods from the industrialized regions of the north central USSR to the north. The report's authors proposed three stages of construction. The first stage would require the blocking of the Neva River and would be the cheapest stage, requiring no more than 20 million rubles. The second stage required the blocking of the Skvira River (by construction of two hydroelectric power stations) that would allow access

2. I. S. Isakov, "Belomorsko-Baltiyskaya Vodnaya Magistral," *Izbrannye Trudy* (Moscow, 1984), pp. 490–498.

3. Istoria Otkritia i Osvoenia Morskogo Severnogo Puti, t.Sh.L. 1959, pp. 31–33.

of ships to Lake Onega and would permit shipment of timber and other cargo from Mariinsk and Leningrad to a new port in Vyterg. Considering the large scope of hydraulic engineering, the cost of the second stage was estimated at 77 million rubles. The third stage, consisting of building a sea canal from Povenets to Soroki and a seaport in Soroki, would be the most expensive at 253 million rubles. The authors emphasized that the last (northern) portion of the canal had not been studied intensively, and therefore the final cost of the project could increase.[4] Thus as of the spring of 1930, the cost of a White Sea–Baltic Canal was estimated at a minimum of 350 million rubles.

The Council of Labor and Defense proposed to create a special committee, headed by Politburo member Ia. E. Rudzutak and including G. G. Yagoda, the deputy minister of the OGPU. This special committee formed a construction administration, subordinate to the transport ministry, to design and construct the southern section of a waterway, but the fate of the northern track (i.e., the canal itself) remained unclear. Despite this uncertainty, the construction administration began its work in the 1929–30 plan year. On May 5, 1930, their draft report was discussed at a meeting of the Politbboro, whose reaction was ambiguous with divergent opinions expressed on the project's advisability and practicality. During the Politburo discussion, notes were exchanged between Stalin and Molotov. Stalin wrote: "I think that it can be constructed up to the Onega. But as to the Northern track, let us limit it to an investigation. I mean it should be constructed mainly by the OGPU. Simultaneously, it is necessary to recalculate the costs for the first part of the construction; 20 million plus 70 million is too much." Molotov's reply summed up the main doubts of the other Politburo members: "I doubt the expediency of the canal. I have read your note, but the

4. GARF 9414.1.1806: 2.

economic part is not clear. Maybe we should consider redrafting."[5] It is worthy of note that at the first discussion of the canal project, Stalin had concluded that the canal should be built by the OGPU— that is, by prison labor.

The skepticism of Molotov was clear. In comparison with the detailed and lucid strategic-military section of the draft, the economic blueprints were not specific. The authors considered only two economic benefits: the increase in timber exports and the opening of better supply routes to Siberia. The lack of precision in economic effects was to be expected because, by the end of the 1920s, northern economic development remained in its infancy. As of 1930 only the Kola Peninsula's mining industrial complex was under construction.

During later Politburo meetings, the supporters of the canal, including Stalin, prevailed and planning continued, though with major compromises to appease the opposition. Construction was planned to begin on the southern part of the canal, from Leningrad to the Onega Lake, in the following economic year. Cost estimates were cut by one-third on the condition that "the total cost of construction of the Southern track not exceed 60 million rubles." Northern construction would be researched but, to cut costs, designers should "take into account any opportunity to use prison labor."[6] The northern track region was unpopulated and required colonization. The lack of infrastructure would raise the cost of hired labor excessively.

The official decree issued by the Committee of Labor and Defense mandated that construction commence on June 3, 1930. The decree reads as follows:

> The Committee of Labor and Defense decrees that: 1. The construction of the White Sea–Baltic Canal is planned. 2. The trans-

---

5. *Pisma I. V. Stalina V. M. Molotovu 1925–1936gg. Sbornik Dokumentov* (Moscow, 1995), pp. 214–215.
     6. Ibid., 214.

port ministry is obliged to start technical research, cost calculation, construction schedules of the whole canal, and preparation of a report for the Commission for Labor and Defense through Gosplan by Sept. 1. Southern construction should begin on October 1, 1930, and should take two years. All the necessary construction facilities will not exceed 60 million rubles and will follow the scheduled guidelines of the years 1930/1931. The geological and technical research of the northern track will be done in cooperation with the military department and the OGPU.

The number of members of the design team, including new experts and OGPU personnel, grew steadily. At the end of May 1930, the Administration of the White Sea–Baltic Canal (later renamed Belomor) began its work on Myasnitskaya Street in Moscow. As its work progressed, the design team had to grapple with a number of problems.

The first stage of construction was to provide a sluice on the Neva River, and the second stage was to provide locks on the Svir River. Simultaneous design work was begun on both projects in order to meet the tight two-year deadline. For a deep-water canal, it was necessary to build three dams equipped with sluices for deep-water ships, but the preparatory work revealed that the planned depth of eighteen feet could not be achieved in only two years. An accelerated plan of action was proposed that would require "a significant quantity of our own and imported equipment." A list of equipment requirements was formulated with the idea of bringing petitions to the respective building organizations for purchasing equipment abroad or for initiating manufacture in domestic factories. The long list of equipment requirements disclosed that the southern waterway was in a financial trap. Equipment purchases and substantial import requirements would raise the cost well in excess of the 60-million-ruble budget.

The first results of research on the more costly northern track were reported at the end of August. Research began on June 14, 1930, when three hundred technical engineers and six hundred workers arrived "to explore an area that lacked realistic maps and to make general geological research for use in designing both economic and technical elements."[7] The team's task was to consider a western deep-water variant and an alternative route that had lower water accumulation in its basin and needed less excavation work, thus saving tens of millions of rubles. Overall, the designers envisioned the building of a huge waterway designed for deep-draft ships. In the south, the locking of the Svir River and the deepening of its channel could be accomplished, but the construction of the locks on the Svir required enormous numbers of qualified personnel, and dredging required 30 caravans of dredge ships at an added cost of 46 million rubles.[8] At the beginning of 1931, only 144 dredge ships were available in the entire Soviet Union to work on internal canals, and new ships were not being produced. These obstacles cast doubt on the feasibility of the schedule (completion by 1932) and of the budget. The total cost was estimated at 353 million rubles, including the northern track that, in itself, cost 321 million rubles. The project cost included the expenses for dredging and excavation equipment (the 30 dredgers and excavators that were not being produced in the USSR). These expenses alone totaled 45 million rubles, 25 million of which were required for the first year.[9] The projected cost of the canal had therefore increased from the 60 million allotted for the southern route alone to 353 million rubles.[10]

The increasing design difficulties and increases in cost estimates aroused skepticism among top Soviet leaders. A letter from Stalin to Molotov dated September 7, 1930, stated that, "I heard Rykov

7. GARF 9414.1.1806: 28.
8. GARF 9414.1.1806: 30.
9. GARF 9414.1.1806: 21–25.
10. To provide a frame of reference, 353 million rubles constituted 20 percent of the 1930 investments in transportation.

and Kviring want to halt the progress of the Northern canal despite the decision of the Politburo. Therefore it is necessary to attack and punish them. It is also necessary to reduce the finance plan to a minimum."[11] Stalin insisted on continuing the project using domestic resources and cited strategic-military considerations, using the support of the military to bolster his case. The transfer of naval forces around Scandinavia was extremely difficult without extensive time for preparation. In the absence of a canal, the military argued that a separate northern naval force was required. The navy would gain considerable new flexibility if it could transfer ships by way of an inland waterway. But the military transfer of submarines, guard ships, and destroyers required a substantial depth on the Svir lock to avoid the necessity of removing arms, ammunition, and fuel to reduce the draft of the ships.

On November 29, 1930, the deputy director of the Gulag, Y. Rappoport, and his chief assistant sent a report to the deputy minister of the OGPU and head of the canal project, Yagoda, warning of complications in dredging the whole canal and calling for the use of only Gulag prisoners. Before this report, only construction of the northern track was intended to be carried out by prison labor, and the rest by free labor. The decision to use forced labor throughout the entire construction of the canal did not solve all financial problems because the Gulag did not have canal equipment. Moreover, the OGPU lacked skilled labor. It had only two dredge engineers, eight to ten technicians, and ten to fifteen excavators among its prisoners. The report's authors suggested that "a few skilled workers be arrested," but even then, there would still be a shortage of skilled personnel.

After analyzing the project proposals, the government made a final decision to proceed with canal construction. The Labor and

11. *Pisma I. V. Stalina V. M. Molotovu 1925–1936 gg. Sbornik dokumentov* (Moscow, 1995), p. 214.

Defense Council decided, among other things, the following: The depth of the White Sea–Baltic Canal was set at ten to twelve feet (instead of eighteen); the canal was to be completed by late 1932; the project would cost no more than 60 to 70 million rubles; and no currency would be allotted to purchase equipment abroad. Unstated, but understood, was the fact that the canal would be built with prison labor. These requirements were difficult to fulfill, since prisoners were designing the canal structures, and they lacked skilled technical and engineering experience. Among them, a professor, V. N. Maslov, created a unique wooden sluice gate capable of maintaining the multiple pressures of the water. This and all the other structures were to be built using local materials and with little use of steel and concrete. The schedule called for intense work, with prisoners working up to sixteen hours a day. On July 1, the project draft was ready, and the Special Committee approved it the very same day. In its final version, the design provided for a transport route of 227 kilometers, 128 hydraulic structures, 19 sluices, and 49 dams. The final estimated cost was 88 million rubles,[12] well below the 353 million originally estimated by civilian planners.

With the project's approval, the Special Committee ordered the beginning of construction. The OGPU began a massive transfer of prisoners, making its correctional labor camp the largest supplier of workers. In mid-1931, according to the report from Yagoda, the number of prisoners rose to more than 100,000 from 72,000 and continued to grow. In 1931, a total of 1,438, or 2 percent of the annual average number of prisoners, died. The death rate rose toward the end of the year because of the increasing industrial losses and deteriorating food supply. A letter from Yagoda to Stalin and Molotov, dated December 31, 1933, explained the reasons for the sharp rise in the death rate. It spoke, among other difficulties, of the

12. GARF 5446.12a.1065: 66.

Table 8.1   Food Supplies for Prisoners, 1932 and 1933 (kg)

Name of the product	Norms in 1932 (Monthly)	Norms in 1933 (Monthly)
Flour	23.5	17.16
Oats	5.75	2.25
Macaroni	0.5	0.4
Vegetable oil	1.0	0.3
Adipose	0.15	presumed zero
Sugar	0.95	0.6
Confectionery products	0.5	0.5
Different canned food (in cans)	2 cans	presumed zero

insufficient supply of food. Table 1 shows the changes in food rations in 1933 as compared with 1932.

This sharp decline in the food supply weakened prisoners especially in spring, when the danger of beriberi was greater. Spring floods and accidents associated with the building of large structures were added causes of the rising death rate during the spring.

Work on the canal required considerable innovation because of the lack of equipment. Engineers improvised waterproof screens, allowing materials to be separated and water to flow freely. Wooden barrow trucks, ironically called "Fords," were created by skilled prisoners to remove stones from trenches. The camp also mastered the use of primitive wooden derrick furnaces to melt iron and steel. They produced more than a thousand tons of home-produced iron to manufacture other necessary materials. Prisoners were organized into brigades and phalanxes. A brigade consisted of 25 to 30 manual laborers, including diggers, fitters, and wheelbarrowers. A phalanx consisted of 250 to 300 men and carried out complex tasks.

Prisoner motivation played a large role in achieving goals and meeting norms. Besides intangible incentives (honorary banners, gratitude, and diplomas), material incentives were also used. Those with exemplary performance received supplementary rations (up to twelve hundred grams of bread), a bonus dish (usually consisting of pies with cabbage or potatoes), and other material awards. The most effective motivator was work credits given to reduce the term of sentence. Refusal to work or falsification of industrial indices (called *tufta* in camp slang), called for punishments including food reduction, intensified supervision, work-credit cancellation, and possibly prosecution.

By the beginning of 1933, most canal structures were completed, but "gaps," such as the watersheds between Vodlozero and Matkozero, remained. Spring floods threatened to break dams and damage canal structures if the gaps were not closed. Work was accelerated, and sporadic efforts were made to complete the watershed. On May 28, 1933, the canal was opened, even though still incomplete. The steamship *Chekist* led the first caravan. The White Sea–Baltic Canal was finished, costing 101 million rubles compared with the estimated cost of 88 million rubles. The first group of ships of the Baltic Fleet made their first transfer on the canal and arrived on July 21, 1933, at Sorokskaia Bay, thereby creating the core of the Northern Military Fleet.

AN EVALUATION

The capacity of the White Sea–Baltic Canal was grossly underused before the war. In 1940 the total transportation volume was one million tons, only 44 percent of the design capacity. The economic importance of the waterway remained insignificant (see Chapter 9). However, the strategic-military importance of the canal was a different story. Before the beginning of World War II, seventeen transfers occurred using the canal and including an array of ships, such as destroyers, submarines, and guard ships. Although Chapter 3 emphasizes the difficulty of moving naval ships through the canal, this view was not shared by the USSR's allies and enemies. Western military intelligence realized the importance of the canal for the defense of the USSR. In 1940 when England and France were preparing to land in the northern area of the USSR to assist Finland, they insisted on capturing and using the canal to capture Leningrad. All the operative plans of the Finnish army provided for the capture or disabling of the canal because it was considered "the main support" of the Soviet regime in Karelia. In May of 1941, a German naval attaché worried that the canal could link the Russian Baltic and other northern fleets. It is unclear whether the Soviet Union's actual and potential military opponents overestimated the importance of the canal, but in any case, they considered it an essential part of the USSR's naval military power.

The fact that the Gulag designed and built the White Sea–Baltic Canal on time and on budget had an enormous effect on the Gulag's development. Large infrastructure projects scheduled for construction by civilian ministries were turned over to the Gulag. By the mid-1930s, the Gulag was the Soviet Union's largest construction organization. The Soviet dictatorship felt justified in its conclusion that prison labor offered a mobile and cheap solution to the nation's infrastructure problems.

The Gulag
in Karelia
1929 to 1941

Christopher Joyce

THE KARELIA REGION was known for its wide-scale use of penal labor. In the 1920s, several escapees from the Solovetskii Islands published vivid accounts of the Soviet penal system.[1] In the early 1930s the Soviet authorities openly publicized their use of penal labor in the construction of the White Sea–Baltic Canal. Thereafter a veil of secrecy descended on the Gulag in Karelia, which would remain undisturbed until the opening of local and regional Soviet archives in the early 1990s.

In Karelia this process was spearheaded by the Institute of Language, Literature, and History, a branch of the Russian Academy of Sciences, and in particular by Vasilii Makurov, who edited a fascinating collection of archival documents on the Gulag in Karelia in the 1930s.[2] Using recently declassified documents from local and central party and government archives, we can create a new per-

1. See S. A. Malsagoff, *An Island Hell: A Soviet Prison in the Far North* (London: A. M. Philpott, 1926); J. D. Bessonov, *My Twenty-six Prisons and My Escape from Solovetsk* (London: J. Cape, 1928); I. M. Zaitsev, *Solovki* (Shanghai: Slovo, 1931).
2. V. G. Makurov (ed.), *Gulag v Karelii, 1930–41* (Petrozavodsk: Karel'skii nauchnyi tsentr, 1992).

spective of the Gulag, provided by the very officials who were responsible for its daily operation. The archival documents used in this chapter were written by a wide range of party, state, and NKVD officials. Most were intended only for a select group and contain much candid information about the Gulag in Karelia, showing its unique and defining position in the evolution of the entire Soviet penal system.[3]

THE TRANSPARENT KARELIAN GULAG (PRE–1933)

From the earliest days of the Soviet regime, some form of prison or concentration camp existed in Karelia. During the Civil War, Soviet authorities established concentration camps on the Solovetskii Islands to hold the prisoners considered most hostile to the Bolshevik regime. The OGPU maintained control over these camps throughout the 1920s, and as the number of prisoners grew, the camps spread from the islands onto the littoral areas of the White Sea.

The OGPU remained aloof from the vibrant political and theoretical penal debates of the 1920s, allowing it to develop its own particular penal system within the SLON (Solovetskii Camp of Special Significance), which promoted self-sufficiency and avoided draining resources from security tasks. The apparent low cost of the SLON was increasingly attractive to Soviet authorities, who were faced with an overcrowded and costly penal system. By May 1929, expanding the camps was necessary after a Council of People's Commissars' decree transferred all prisoners serving sentences of more than three years to OGPU jurisdiction.[4]

---

3. C. S. Joyce, "The Gulag 1930–1960: Karelia and the Soviet System of Forced Labor" (Ph.D. diss., University of Birmingham, 2001).

4. Sovnarkom decree July 11, 1929, "Ob ispol'zovanii truda ugolovno-zaklyuchennykh" in M. I. Khlusov (ed.), *Ekonomika Gulaga i ee Rol' v Razvitii*

This transfer of responsibility to the OGPU coincided with a substantial rise in the penal population as a direct result of collectivization. The SLON camps expanded rapidly, peaking in January 1931 with a population of 71,800 prisoners.[5] Most were employed in the timber industry, which was short of labor despite a Western campaign against the dumping of cheap timber produced by penal labor.[6] The most visible penal timber operations were suspended while foreign dignitaries toured the region. Molotov attempted to parry this anti-Soviet campaign by insisting that penal labor be used only on internal infrastructure projects, such as the construction of the White Sea–Baltic (Belomor) Canal.[7]

THE BELOMOR CANAL

The idea of a canal linking the Baltic and White Seas had first been proposed during the eighteenth century, but no practical steps were taken until the Soviet period. To prove the superiority of the Soviet system not only over the previous regime but also over the apparently bankrupt Western capitalist nations, the Soviet authorities decided to construct the Belomor Canal to link the Great Northern

---

Strany—1930-e gody, Sbornik Dokumnetov (Moscow: RAN, 1998), document No. 4. See also documents 1–3.

5. M. B. Smirnov (ed.), *Sistema Ispravitel'no-Trudovykh Lagerei v SSSR - Spravochnik* (Moscow: Zven'ya, 1998), p. 395.

6. For debates on Soviet forced labor at the time, see *Times* (London) May 18–20, 1931; *Daily Mail* (London) February 2, 1931; L. I. Parker, ed., *Forced Labor in Russia: Facts and Documents* (London: British Russian Gazette and Trade Outlook, 1931).

7. In February 1931 both the author George Bernard Shaw and Lady Astor visited the northwestern Russian Republic to verify Molotov's claims that forced labor was not used in the timber industry. During these visits all OGPU timber operations were moved to remote locations and then returned to their original areas of operation once the dignitaries had left. D. J. Dallin and B. I. Nicolaevsky, *Forced Labor in Soviet Russia* (London: Hollis & Carter, 1948), 226.

Route by a network of internal waterways.[8] Not only would this grand construction improve the nation's infrastructure and open up the natural resources of the Karelian region to industrial exploitation, but the use of prisoners would demonstrate the progressive nature of the Soviet corrective-labor penal policy.[9] The initial hyperbole of this portrayal ensured that the project maintained a high profile throughout the construction period, even though access to prisoners and worksites was strictly controlled. Soviet authorities further complicated the project by announcing that the construction would receive minimal funding, would use only local materials, and would be finished in a short period, as is explained in Chapter 8.

These conditions proved impossible to fulfill, and fundamental changes to the canal's specifications were necessary. In February 1931, a secret decree reduced the depth of the northern section of the canal, which had been entrusted to the OGPU, from eighteen feet to twelve feet,[10] transforming the canal from an important transport route to a backwater, suitable only for shallow barges and passenger vessels.[11] Construction on the northern section of the canal was slow, and the pace only quickened after G. Yagoda (dep-

8. The Great Northern Route was an attempt to establish a permanent sea route, together with the appropriate infrastructure, along the entire length of the Soviet northern coastline. Such a navigable route was intended to help the development of Siberian settlements and provide an alternative route to the Far East that would pass solely through Soviet waters.

9. For an example of the portrayal of Soviet superiority, see *Komsomol'skaya Pravda* (Moscow: August 5, 1933), p. 1.

10. STO (Council of Labor and Defense) secret decree No. 4—June 3, 1930, had stated a depth of twenty feet to allow for the passage of vessels with an eighteen-foot draft. The northern section of the canal, which had been assigned to the OGPU, stretched from Povenets on Lake Onega to Belomorsk (Soroka) on the White Sea. Y. Kilin, *Kareliya v politike Sovetskogo gosudarstva, 1920–1941* (Petrozavodsk: State University Press, 1999), p. 127.

11. Report by the Chairman of the Revolutionary Military Council (Revvoensovet). GARF 9414.1.1806: 44. Once the canal was officially opened, it was discovered that on some sections of the River Svir the depth was only six feet, making it inaccessible to *any* vessel in the Baltic Fleet!

uty head of the OGPU) and the Council of People's Commissars ordered the Gulag to make the project a priority at the expense of all other tasks. As a result there was a huge increase in the number of prisoners, and strict military discipline was imposed.[12]

The project was completed quickly despite the harsh weather and the unmechanized methods of work. Great publicity accompanied the canal's opening on June 30, 1933, claiming "an important victory for the USSR on the frontline of industrialization and the strengthening of the defense capability of the nation."[13] In reality the shallow depth of the canal prevented the passage of any vessel from the Baltic fleet, and large cargo shipments had to be reloaded onto smaller craft. As soon as the project was finished, proposals were made for the construction of a second route to allow larger vessels, but to no avail. Even as late as 1939, the first secretary of the Karelian oblast' committee stated that "specialists believe it would be cheaper, quicker and more valuable to build a second canal, parallel to the first at a distance of about 1km to the east, along the entire route."[14] Because of these shortcomings the publicity surrounding the canal faded rapidly, and the whole region was increasingly shrouded in secrecy as the canal and its environs were assigned to the OGPU for further development.

The only agency to benefit from the Belomor project was the Gulag, which had successfully demonstrated the potential of using

12. Between 1931 and 1932, the number of prisoners serving the construction project increased from 64,000 to 99,000, peaking in December 1932 with 108,000. *Sistema Ispravitel'no-Trudovykh Lagerei v SSSR—Spravochnik*, p. 162. Prisoners in Karelia were held in one of two camp systems, the BBLag (White Sea–Baltic Camp) or SLAG (Solovetskii Camp). The SLON camp had been reorganized into three camps in 1929—Visherlag, Svir'lag, and the USiKMITL (the Administration of Solovetskie and Karelo-Murmansk Corrective-Labor Camps). With the start of canal construction, most prisoners from USiKMITL were transferred to a new camp system, the BBLag, and those remaining were entrusted to SLAG (Solovetskii Camp). Ibid., 395.

13. *Gulag v Karelii, 1930–41*, doc. No. 56—July 27, 1933.

14. *Kareliya v politike Sovetskogo gosudarstva, 1920–1941*, p. 127.

penal labor on large-scale construction projects. However, the completion of the canal was only the beginning of the Gulag's involvement in the development of Karelia. Throughout the 1930s this region was a testing ground for the use of penal labor on different projects, and the experience gained in Karelia was soon disseminated throughout the entire Gulag.[15]

THE WHITE SEA–BALTIC COMBINE (BBK)

To make good use of the Gulag's water-engineering skills, the OGPU was given the task of building the Moscow-Volga Canal. Many skilled prisoners were transferred from Karelia to this new project, but a significant number remained in the BBLag (White Sea–Baltic Camp), which was now assigned to the newly created White Sea–Baltic Combine (BBK). The BBK served as a regional developer with exclusive rights to the exploitation of the canal and any natural resources surrounding it,[16] and "no establishment nor individual, without special permission from SNK USSR, [had] the right to interfere in the administrative-economic and operational activities of the combine." The BBK received central funding and was granted tax-free status until January 1, 1936, by which time it was expected to have established a working infrastructure and profitable enterprises.[17] After 1936 there was a noticeable change in the economic activities of the BBK as the combine attempted to achieve

15. On completion of the canal, the Russian republic adopted a new corrective-labor code (August 1, 1933) which incorporated many lessons learned from the Belomor project and stressed the primacy of physical labor as the basis of the Soviet penal system. For a copy of this statute, see A. I. Kokurin and N. V. Petrov, eds., *Gulag 1917–1960* (Moscow: Demokratiya, 2000), Document No. 19; also see Joyce, "The Gulag 1930–1960."

16. *Gulag v Karelii, 1930–1941*, doc. No. 66 (August 17, 1933). The importance of the BBLag was strengthened because the head of the BBLag also served as the deputy head of the Gulag.

17. Ibid.

financial self-sufficiency by divesting itself of unprofitable activities and of the camps associated with them. In 1937 the BBLag was relieved of the added expense of maintaining the Solovetskii Islands as a strict regime camp, and jurisdiction passed to the Main Administration of State Security, which continued to hold the BBlag's high-profile prisoners.

THE SEARCH FOR AN ECONOMIC IDENTITY (1933–37)

The generous financial support granted to the BBK during the second Five-Year Plan allowed the BBK to experiment with different economic activities in an effort to discover which were more suited to the use of forced labor. The experience gained in Karelia had direct relevance to Gulag activities across the Soviet Union.

A successful agricultural base was deemed essential if the combine was to establish a permanent workforce. The Karelian authorities were particularly excited about the establishment of agricultural experimental centers to investigate the prospects for farming in northern climates. The combine was less excited by small-scale local agricultural operations, and although one of its main tasks was supposedly colonization using special settlements, it preferred to focus on large-scale industrial exploitation and construction. As a result agriculture remained unimportant throughout the 1930s and only supplemented imported supplies.[18]

Remote OGPU camps were required to develop a local infrastructure and to erect buildings to meet their needs. The OGPU camps in the Karelian region had enough experience to establish new camps and the auxiliary enterprises needed to keep them operational. Much of this construction was small-scale, but with the

18. Ibid., docs. No. 77, 115. Despite the abundant expanse of water in and around the Karelo-Murmansk region, the combine's attempts at establishing a fishing industry were swiftly curtailed after disastrous results in 1936 when the plan was only fulfilled by 5.6 percent. GARF 9414.1.844: l. 4, 20.

completion of the canal the forced laborers of the Gulag had proved that they were capable of finishing important capital construction projects. The variety of capital projects assigned to the BBK encompassed the complete range of construction tasks entrusted to the Gulag during the prewar years.

The construction of a hydroelectric power station (Tulomstroi) on the river Tuloma, near Murmansk, dominated the combine's activities for the period of the second Five-Year Plan. On completion in 1937, Tulomstroi became the most northerly power station in the world. Its generating capacity could meet the power requirements for Murmansk and for the Kola Peninsula and the Kirov railway line. Tulomstroi became a semiautonomous agency within the combine and received priority for all supplies and labor. Although the BBK directed considerable time and resources toward the Tulomstroi project, the combine received no benefit from its completion. Unlike the Belomor Canal, the Tuloma power station was transferred to a civilian agency once it became operational, and all the resources assigned to the project were sent to other pressing NKVD projects instead of to the combine as expected.[19]

During the Yagoda and Yezhov periods, most Gulag construction focused on the development of a working infrastructure to support the primary planned economic task for that region. Large-scale construction only occurred when the completed enterprise would form the backbone of plans for the future assimilation of the area, as was true for the Norilsk nickel combine or the timber-paper-chemical combine, which was located in the Karelian town of Segezha and assigned to a quasi-independent agency (Segezhstroi) in the BBK.[20] However, the BBK had learned from the Tulomstroi experience not to concentrate its resources on specific tasks at the

19. GARF 9414.1.954: 4.
20. NKVD order No. 348—November 10, 1935, GARF 9401.1.

expense of all other activities, particularly without guarantees that a completed project would stay in their jurisdiction.

Segezhstroi experienced difficulties from its inception, plagued by problems with supplies and labor and by the discovery, at the end of 1935, that the local administration had not only been using different plan headings from those used by the central Gulag authorities, but was actually working from a completely different plan![21] After the first stage of Segezhstroi was finished in March 1939, construction on the rest of the project faltered as resources were diverted to other pressing tasks.[22]

The BBK increasingly insulated itself from financial and organizational problems in Segezhstroi by emphasizing its administrative independence. In October 1939 the BBLag camp district serving Segezhstroi became a camp in its own right (Segezhlag) and was assigned to the now truly autonomous construction project.[23]

Although manufacturing received little publicity, it was a benefit to the combine as a whole. These industries (sewing, leather-processing, fur-farming, woodworking) met much of the internal demand within the local Gulag and also employed many weak prisoners whose presence on other tasks would have hindered work. Manufacturing was profitable and by 1939 provided as much as 31 percent of the combine's total income, even though more than 80 percent of resources were devoted to activities requiring heavy phys-

21. GARF 9414.1.764: 3–3ob.

22. This lack of support from the central Gulag authorities for the further development of Segezhstroi was surprising since cellulose production was particularly important to the explosives industry. Elsewhere, the Gulag was developing other cellulose plants (e.g., Arkhangel'sk oblast') and had created the Cellulose-Paper Department to assist in the construction and operation of such enterprises. Perhaps the close proximity of Segezha to the Finnish border made any further expansion unwise. NKVD order No. 00366, GARF 9401.1.

23. NKVD order No. 001273—October 21, 1939, Central State Archive of Crimean Republic (Tsentralnyi Gosudarstvennyi Arkhiv Respublici Krym, hereafter—TsGARK), f. 865, op. 35, sv. 1, d. 2a, l. 314.

ical labor.[24] Despite their economic success, these industries were regarded as auxiliary activities, and the BBK devoted more attention to high-profile, large-scale projects, which were considered more suitable to penal labor.

Unlike other infrastructure projects, the Belomor Canal remained in Gulag jurisdiction since it would become a major new water route and was supposed to facilitate the industrial assimilation of central Karelia. The depth of the canal required that most cargo be reloaded onto smaller barges built by the combine itself. Cargo turnover did increase, but toward the late 1930s it became apparent that most shipments originated, or were destined for, locations in central Karelia and that the canal was mainly used as a private transport route for the combine.[25] Eventually, all parties, including the BBK, accepted that the combine's control of the canal was of benefit to no one, and the canal was transferred to the Peoples' Commissariat for Water Transport in April 1939.[26] This experience may have convinced both the Gulag and the government that penal labor was more suited to primary industries, and as a result the Gulag was never again entrusted with the administration of a major transport route.

During the first Five-Year Plan, Gulag timber operations were uncoordinated and were engaged either in contract work for local timber organizations or preparatory work for the development of future NKVD regions. Toward the end of the second Five-Year Plan, timber activities increased as it became apparent that they were suited to the growing pool of unskilled manual labor. The BBK and BBLag were at the forefront of the expanding Gulag timber activities and dominated this penal activity for the rest of the 1930s. Much

24. Joyce, "The Gulag 1930–1960," 102–103.
25. Ibid., 117–118.
26. SNK USSR decree No. 321—March 23, 1939, NKVD order No. 079—April 5, 1939, GARF 9414.1.

of the expansion in the combine's timber industry was at the expense of Karelian timber organizations, which lacked the BBK's endless supply of labor and political support. By 1937 the combine was producing 35 percent of cut timber and 12 percent of sawn timber in Karelia, a substantial achievement for such a new organization.[27]

LOCAL CONFLICT

The growth of the Gulag in Karelia led to increasing friction with the local authorities. During the 1920s, OGPU activities were welcomed by the local government since prisoners were employed in sparsely populated regions lacking a permanent workforce. Relations between the Gulag and the Karelian authorities began to deteriorate, however, during the construction of the Belomor Canal. The Karelian government appreciated the effect the canal would have on the region, but despite their continual offers of assistance and pleas for information, they were largely ignored by the OGPU.[28] Communication between the Gulag and local authorities was almost nonexistent, and the arrogant behavior of the OGPU-NKVD toward the Karelian government continued throughout the 1930s. When the BBK was granted control over vast areas of central Karelia, the Karelian government lost control overnight of the resources and industries in this region and faced a constant struggle against the further expansion of Gulag activities. Questions of colonization, defense, transport, infrastructure, local hydrology, and so on, were increasingly decided by the secretive OGPU-NKVD, whose line of command went straight to Moscow, bypassing local authorities.

27. V. G. Makurov, "Belomorsko-Baltiiskii kombinat v Karelii, 1933–1941," *Novoe v izuchenie istorii Karelii* (Petrozavodsk: 1994), p. 158.

28. Even those Karelian officials co-opted onto official supervisory bodies were generally sidelined. The chairman of the special committee overseeing the Belomor project did not realize for eight months that the chairman of the Karelian SNK (E. Gyulling) was also a member of the committee. GARF 9414.1.1805: 84.

The coordination between the BBK and local government was minimal, plunging development plans into confusion. At the start of the second Five-Year Plan, the Karelian republic was subject to four different plan variants, produced by the Karelian planning agency, the Gosplan USSR, the Leningrad oblast, and the BBK—but the plans were not integrated. Each of these bodies had received funding dependent on the plans. The government of Karelia, supposedly an autonomous republic, had no control or even knowledge of the investment decisions made about its own territory. The BBK area, in particular, had been taken away from the jurisdiction of the Karelian government; the republic had lost control of the heart of its territorial integrity.[29]

ECONOMIC SPECIALIZATION (1937–41)

The BBK-BBLag remained the most powerful combine-camp system in Karelia throughout the 1930s, but during the third Five-Year Plan its supremacy was challenged by events both inside and outside the republic. With the creation of Tulomstroi and Segezhstroi, the combine had encouraged the establishment of independent camp systems to finish large new construction tasks. This tendency grew in 1939 and 1940 when several urgent projects in the region were assigned to the Gulag, which created new camps for each of these tasks, bypassing involvement by the BBK.[30] These developments were welcomed by the BBK-BBLag under the leadership of M. M.

---

29. *Kareliya v politike Sovetskogo gosudarstva, 1920–1941*, p. 136. On some occasions the Karelian authorities did manage to outmaneuver the Gulag, the most notable example being the construction of two railway lines (Dorstroi 1 and 2), where the BBK continually sought plan details from the Karelian Peoples' Commissariat for the Timber Industry, details which were not forthcoming. For more on this subject, see Joyce, "The Gulag 1930–1960," 100–101.

30. Other camps created include Segzhlag, Kandalakshlag, Matkozhlag, Keksgol'mlag, Monchegorlag.

Timofeev, who wanted to focus on logging and timber processing.[31] The move to economic specialization in the BBK-BBLag was soon mirrored across the Gulag with the establishment of NKVD economic administrations dedicated to specific kinds of production. The BBLag became the most important camp in the Gulag for Timber Processing (ULLP).

The arrival of Timofeev marked a distinct change in the operation of the BBK and BBLag and presaged the future transformation of the Gulag under the direction of L. Beria. By 1937 the combine was just beginning to discover which economic activities were most profitable when the NKVD embarked on its frenzied purge, depriving the Gulag of leadership and direction. Even the Gulag was not immune from the Great Terror, and in 1938 several high-ranking BBK personnel were arrested for having links with "enemies of the people," an accusation hard to parry when working in an organization that dealt with "counterrevolutionaries"![32] The prisoners were also subject to renewed investigations and arrests, and between 1937 and 1939, hundreds of inmates from the BBLag and the Solovetskii Islands were executed en masse.[33] The disruption and distrust created by this maelstrom only began to be rectified in the BBK and BBLag with the arrival of Timofeev, who was determined to transform the combine into a profitable timber agency.[34] The Gulag

31. M. M. Timofeev was head of both the BBK and BBLag from August 28, 1937, to March 1, 1941. *Sistema ispravitel'no-trudovykh lagerei v SSSR—Spravochnik*, p. 163.

32. *Gulag v Karelii, 1930–1941*, doc. No. 122.

33. Between October 27 and November 4, 1937, a total of 1,111 prisoners were executed at Sandormokh, a remote, forested area six kilometers west of Povenets (site of the first lock-gate into the Belomor Canal from Lake Onega) and twelve kilometers east of Medvezh'egorsk (location of the headquarters of the BBK and BBLag). I. I. Chukhin, *Kareliya—37: ideologiya i praktika terrora* (Petrozavodsk: State University, 1999), pp. 124–125.

34. It is ironic that Timofeev, who was instrumental in creating a profitable combine, used economic arguments in his campaign to discredit both Pliner (head of Gulag 1937–1938) and Yagoda (NKVD 1934–1936), claiming that they

system had paid little attention to establishing a stable local work-force. Under Timofeev's leadership, attempts were made to stabilize the camp workforce by preventing the mass seasonal movement of prisoners. Kinds of production were organized to allow exploitation throughout the year, and each work site was allotted a basic number of workers.[35] Having limited the number of workers who could be freely transferred, Timofeev introduced training courses to improve productivity, since there was no fear of losing these trained workers to another camp system. He also imposed greater central control over camp districts *(lagotdeleniya)* and camp compounds *(lag-punkty)* to limit friction between outposts in the BBLag.[36] Although his actions improved productivity, Timofeev was unable to completely alter the emphasis on fulfilling only short-term goals, since most local officials were well aware of the potentially lethal recriminations that could arise from failure.

---

exploited the Gulag as an economic agency rather than treated it as a penal institution. *Gulag v Karelii, 1930–1941*, doc. No. 130.

35. For example, the timber section of the BBK administration was upgraded into a Department of the Timber Industry, which was granted a fixed number of *zeks* who could not be transferred to nontimber work without the permission of the department. TsGARK, f. 865, op. 35, sv. 2, d. 5, l. 12 (March 23, 1939).

36. In an attempt to improve the flow of information within the BBK, the combine established its own communication network independent of any Karelian infrastructure. Once completed, this network was able to reach every camp location, narrow-gauge railway, ice-dirt road in the BBK's area of operations. (TsGARK, f. 865, op. 36, sv. 3, d. 30, l. 91). Timofeev was not completely successful in eradicating bad practices from the BBLag. In BBK directive No. 06200, December 28, 1940, he complained that despite six orders issued by the combine leadership in the past eighteen months, some heads of camp districts were still transferring prisoners within the system without letting the central BBLag authorities know. Such actions ensured that the central accounts were inaccurate and that the leadership would lose track of the actual number and location of prisoners in its system. (TsGARK, f. 865, op. 35, sv. 3, d. 13—1940).

THE WINTER WAR

By the late 1930s the international situation had deteriorated, and the Soviet government was increasingly concerned about Karelia's extensive border with Finland. In 1939 the Soviet General Staff reported that Finland had sixty airbases and landing strips while in the area stretching from Lake Ladoga to the Barents Sea, the Red Army did not have a single aerodrome.[37] The only organization in the region with substantial labor and material resources at its disposal was the BBK-BBLag, which were soon entrusted with the construction of numerous defense works.[38] After it became apparent that the Soviet authorities had underestimated the tenacity of Finnish forces, BBLag prisoners were dispatched to construct defense works throughout Karelia and Murmansk, and timber production and manufacturing were reconfigured to meet the demands of these new construction projects.[39] The BBLag was instructed to relocate all prisoners sentenced as "counterrevolutionaries" (about thirty thousand people) away from the Belomor Canal, the Kirov railway line, and other strategic points, even though such locations were generally at the heart of the BBK economic operations.[40] Even camps deep in the forest had to curtail lumbering to meet the strict blackout

37. *Kareliya v politike Sovetskogo gosudarstva, 1920–1941*, p. 121.

38. Even as late as November 1939 (i.e., the month the Winter War began) there were still no antiaircraft defenses or artillery posts along the Belomor Canal. Archive of Social and Political Movements and Formations of the Republic of Karelia (AOPDFRK), f. 3, op. 65, d. 10, l. 16, 47.

39. The BBLag sent four thousand prisoners to project No. 100, the construction of the Petrozavodsk-Suoyarvi road, and sixteen thousand prisoners to project No. 105, the construction of a railway line around Kandalaksha. TsGARK, f. 865, op. 36, sv. 3, d. 24, l. 2-4.

40. This order was given on November 26, 1939, and stated that all transfers should be completed in the next three days, that is, before hostilities began. The order provides further evidence that the Soviet declaration of war against Finland was premeditated. TsGARK, f. 865, op. 36, sv. 3, d. 30, l. 91–92.

regulations, although several camps flouted this ruling, and some were even accused of using higher-wattage bulbs than normal![41]

Even with the cessation of hostilities with Finland during the short interlude between the Winter War and the Great Patriotic War, most prisoners sent to complete defense works were not returned but were transferred to new projects that arose from the assimilation of Finnish territories ceded to the Soviet Union by the Treaty of Moscow. The rapid advances of German and Finnish forces in 1941 forced the mass evacuation of both camp and combine, although some prisoners did remain behind to finish urgent tasks.[42]

SECURITY, ORDER, AND HEALTH

The remoteness of the Solovetskii Islands was suited to the isolation of prisoners considered hostile to the Bolshevik regime. The expansion of Gulag activities onto the Karelian mainland throughout the 1930s and the growing integration of forced labor with the mainstream economy meant that previous levels of security were no longer possible. Attempts were made to prevent "anti-Soviet" elements from mixing with the local population and holding positions of responsibility in the camp administration, but "counterrevolutionaries" were usually the best-qualified prisoners to hold administrative posts as the Gulag economy diversified. The use of such prisoners in the administration was tacitly accepted and occasionally even encouraged. In June 1939 the deputy head of the BBLag, N. S. Levinson, called on all sections of the camp to employ prisoners with accounting experience in their accounting departments, even if the prisoners included "counterrevolutionaries."[43] This

41. TsGARK, f. 865, op. 35, sv. 3, d. 14, l. 59.
42. For more details on the use of prisoners in Karelia during the Great Patriotic War see Joyce, "The Gulag 1930–1960."
43. TsGARK, f. 865, op. 35, sv. 1, d. 1, l. 120.

order was in response to threats by the state bank (Gosbank) to impose sanctions if the BBLag did not produce correct and full financial accounts. The following year, after the theft of 120,000 rubles led to an investigation of the BBLag administration, Levinson was apparently surprised to discover that many "counterrevolutionaries" occupied administrative posts.[44] After such revelations, these prisoners were removed from their posts but were usually reinstated as soon as the furor had died down.

Once Beria took control of the NKVD, genuine attempts were made to reduce the number of prisoners, especially "counterrevolutionaries," employed by the Gulag administration. The growth of a permanent Gulag cadre under Beria facilitated the removal of prisoners from the administration, although many of the "free worker" replacements were actually former prisoners, some of them former "counterrevolutionaries."[45]

The use of prisoners in the day-to-day running of the Gulag was especially prevalent for camp guards. The post of camp guard was unappealing because of the poor working and living conditions and the dangers posed by criminal elements among the camp population.[46] As a result, the camp authorities were compelled to use prisoners to staff positions that remained vacant. Between June 1936 and July 1938, about half the guards in the BBLag were prisoners, but this proportion fell gradually after the arrival of Timofeev, and by April 1941 only 2 percent of guards were prisoners.[47] This significant change in the guards was mirrored across the Soviet Union

44. TsGARK, f. 865, op. 35, sv. 3, d. 13, l. 93ob.

45. On January 1, 1940, 29 percent of the BBLag administrative staff were former prisoners, including 8 percent former "counterrevolutionaries." TsGARK, f. 865, op. 32, sv. 1, d. 5, l. 78–78ob.

46. For examples of the poor conditions endured by free worker guards, which often led to poor morale, drunkenness, and even suicide, see *Gulag v Karelii, 1930–1941*, doc. No. 136; TsGARK, f. 865, op. 35, sv. 1, d. 1a, l. 32–35.

47. *Gulag v Karelii, 1930–1941*, doc. No. 103; TsGARK, f. 865, op. 32, sv. 1, d. 10, l. 71–71ob, TsGARK, f. 865, op. 32, sv. 3, d. 27, l. 2–16.

as Beria sought to improve the working conditions of NKVD employees.

During the 1920s the penal population of the SLON contained several cohesive prisoner groups based on former political allegiances or religious convictions. On certain dates, such as workers' holidays or religious feasts, these groups staged protests against Soviet power and against their conditions of imprisonment. By the 1930s such cohesive groups no longer existed, yet the BBLag and other camps continued to prevent prisoners from going to work on these days, and extremely detailed security arrangements were in effect for the period of the holiday.[48] No real threat to security in the BBLag ever materialized from the prisoners, but this did not prevent overzealous security agencies from "exposing" pernicious plots. In 1933 the OGPU "discovered" a "counterrevolutionary, insurrectional organization of prisoners" that was planning to tear the Karelian republic from the Soviet Union and give both it and the Belomor Canal to Finland![49]

Apart from spontaneous, isolated incidents, many of which were the result of alcohol, the most serious form of disorder was escape attempts, which always had a potential for the unwelcome involvement of other agencies, particularly if the escapee committed further crimes. Although security around many of the camp compounds was surprisingly lax, both the administration and the prisoners understood that it was extremely difficult to escape in a sparsely populated region littered with NKVD personnel. Although the proportion of inmates escaping from the BBLag was higher than the Gulag average, the high recapture rate meant few prisoners

48. For examples, see TsGARK, f. 865, op. 35, sv. 1, d. 1, l. 300; TsGARK, f. 865, op. 35, sv. 3, d. 9, l. 296–311.
49. I. I. Chukhin, *Kanalarmeitsy* (Petrozavodsk: 1990), pp. 193–200. In fact this accusation merely provided additional material for a campaign against ethnic Finns living in Karelia.

remained at large.[50] Nevertheless, the BBLag was criticized for its poor security, which failed to improve significantly despite claims to the contrary made by Timofeev.[51] At the local level BBLag officials sacrificed security issues to ensure uninterrupted production. The diversion of limited resources to improve security was opposed by the central camp authorities if it threatened economic plan goals.

The launch of the Belomor project was accompanied by much publicity about the progressive nature of the Soviet penal system and its use of the labor process to reform prisoners. The process of reeducating offenders, known as *perekovka* (reforging), was entrusted to the Cultural Education Department (Kul'turno-vospitatel'nyi otdel—KVO), which was supposed to instill an enthusiastic work ethic, supported by cultural and educational activities. This work was highly politicized and needed a significant number of Party workers. The KVO was considered an extremely unattractive post, however, and the department experienced severe staff shortages even during the high-profile canal construction. Consequently, some local officials were forced to use prisoners to fill many posts. In the fourth camp district of the SLAG (Solovetskii Camp) only 97 of 129 KVO posts were filled in 1931. Of these workers, 25 were prisoners sentenced for "counterrevolutionary" crimes and ought not to have been involved in the political reeducation of other inmates.[52]

On completion of the canal, many party workers employed in the BBLag moved on to the Moscow-Volga Canal, leaving behind a staff of questionable quality. The Gulag's penal system was increasingly shrouded in secrecy as Soviet propaganda focused on Nazi Germany and its concentration camps. At the local level, most in the KVO paid lip service to political indoctrination, and the

50. See tables in Joyce, "The Gulag 1930–1960," 130.
51. NKVD order No. 001408—November 6, 1940 (GARF, f. 9401, op. 1).
52. *Gulag v Karelii, 1930–1941*, doc. No. 8.

department was mainly involved in schemes to boost productivity or to provide cultural activities. Unlike many other camp systems, the BBLag provided its prisoners with a wide range of cultural activities, many of which it had inherited from the rich cultural and academic life of the Solovetskii camps during the 1920s. The close proximity of Karelia to Leningrad ensured that its penal population included intellectuals and performing artists, who gave high-quality productions for prisoners and local civilians. The BBLag even had a theater, located in Medvezh'egorsk, which employed 338 people, most of them prisoners.[53] However, in 1939, in an attempt to improve security and reduce the profile of prisoners, all prisoners were removed from performing roles, although they were still allowed to play in the orchestra and work as set designers and builders and costume-makers.[54] Some attempts were made to improve the education of prisoners by campaigns to eradicate illiteracy, but the constant transfer of prisoners between camps severely disrupted such work.

The basis of the *perekovka* principle was the proviso that prisoners should be provided with a set standard of living conditions that met their basic needs, allowing them to concentrate on their own redevelopment. If conditions fell below this standard, it was considered harmful to the prisoners' reeducation. Yet even during the Belomor period, the head of the Gulag, L. I. Kogan, was forced to remind the BBLag leadership that "the men [prisoners] and their comforts are every bit as important as the obligatory fulfillment of the production programme." Surprisingly, this order and other allusions to poor living conditions are frequently mentioned in M. Gorky's book on the Belomor Canal, and it is not clear whether this

53. For further details on theater in the BBK, see M. M. Korallova (ed.), *Teatr Gulaga* (Moscow: Memorial, 1995).
54. TsGARK, f. 865, op. 35, sv. 2, d. 4, l. 37. The BBLag theater was destroyed by Finnish forces during the Great Patriotic War.

situation was ever rectified. In 1933 the deputy head of the OGPU, Yagoda, issued a similar order, although the emphasis was then placed on providing living conditions that would maintain a prisoner's labor productivity rather than providing opportunities for reeducation.[55]

Living conditions across the Gulag deteriorated and reached a low point during the purges. Once Beria became the people's commissar for internal affairs, attempts were made to improve conditions for prisoners. However, the orders issued by the central Gulag authorities on improvements to living conditions were unrealistic and were rarely accompanied by added funding. In 1939 Timofeev complained to Beria that if he obeyed rules on appropriate winter clothing, as many as fifteen thousand inmates would be confined to barracks. Beria's response was to call for the establishment of workshops where prisoners could repair their clothing, but as no extra funding was provided, few camps heeded this call.[56] Timofeev made many pleas for increases in capital investment for infrastructure. Of 150 camp compounds, only 30 had separate dining rooms, and elsewhere prisoners were forced to eat in their overcrowded barracks.[57]

Gulag medical personnel had to ensure that the greatest number of prisoners were fit for production. Competence was evaluated using death and sickness rates, the number of nonworking and invalid prisoners, and so on. Each camp system could have a certain proportion of its prisoner population excused from work for illness. However, the combination of poor living conditions and heavy

55. *Gulag v Karelii, 1930–1941*, doc. No. 72.

56. NKVD order No. 74—March 3, 1939. TsGARK, f. 865, op. 35, sv. 1, d. 2a, l. 16–18ob.

57. *Gulag v Karelii, 1930–1941*, doc. No. 130. On October 30, 1940, in the seventh transit colony of the BBLag, a tier of bunks was so overloaded that it collapsed and crushed one prisoner to death. NKVD order No. 00297—March 18, 1941–TsGARK, f. 865, op. 35, sv. 3, d. 14.

physical labor ensured that the number of sick prisoners always exceeded the accepted quota. In 1936, the BBK made proposals to establish special groups of weakened prisoners that would receive better rations and accommodations and be gradually reintroduced to work under the supervision of medical personnel.[58] The number of invalids and weak prisoners among the BBLag population grew throughout the 1930s. Timofeev tried to place them in jobs that needed little physical labor, such as the manufacturing sector or the maintenance of camp compounds, but all prisoners, regardless of their health, wanted these less physically demanding jobs. In 1938 it was revealed that of the 7,350 prisoners engaged in camp maintenance in the BBLag, only 1,260 were genuine invalids. The rest, many of whom had secured their positions through bribery and influence, were judged capable of physical labor.[59]

In 1940 Timofeev—who had lost many of his labor-capable prisoners to urgent projects elsewhere in the region—asked the central authorities to recalculate plan figures to take into account the excessive number of invalids in the BBLag workforce.[60] He also appealed for permission to increase the proportion of prisoners allowed to occupy hospital beds. For the first half of 1940, the authorities granted the BBLag 2,041 hospital beds, enough for 3.34 percent of the camp's population, but the weakened health of this workforce and the disruption of food and medical supplies caused by the Winter War had increased the daily number of prisoners needing beds to 2,220.[61]

Even such conclusive data rarely convinced the central authorities to change plan goals, and the only time medical personnel could directly affect production was when an infectious disease threatened

---

58. *Gulag v Karelii, 1930–1941*, doc. No. 100.
59. *Gulag v Karelii, 1930–1941*, doc. No. 133.
60. TsGARK, f. 865, op. 36, sv. 3, d. 24, l. 8. It is not clear whether Timofeev was successful since he was soon promoted to another job.
61. TsGARK, f. 865, op. 36, sv. 3, d. 24, l. 53–54.

Table 9.1   Mortality Rates in the Gulag

Year/Mortality Rate (%)	OGPU/NKVD Camps	BBLag
1931	2.9	2.2
1932	4.8	2.1
1933	15.0	10.5
1934	4.3	2.4
1935	3.6	1.7
1936	2.5	1.7
1937	2.8	3.3
1938	7.8	4.8
1939	3.8	3.0
1940	3.3	2.9

Source: Joyce, "The Gulag 1930–1960: Karelia and the Soviet System of Forced Labor," p. 150.

to reach epidemic levels. In March 1939 the fifth camp district (Nizhne-Vyg) of the BBLag stopped work, and the entire compound was quarantined until medical staff decreed that the epidemic had passed.[62] However, local medical staff, many of whom were prisoners, were under pressure from local camp bosses to prevent any interruption of production, and so serious medical conditions, such as venereal diseases, were ignored unless the level of infection increased rapidly.[63]

The provision of food and medical supplies to the Gulag was subject to the unpredictability of the Soviet planned economy. Prisoners were at the bottom of the national supply chain, and thus any shortages felt throughout society were acutely felt in the Gulag. During the famine in 1933, the mortality rate in the OGPU camps, including even the high-profile BBLag, reached alarming proportions (see Table 9.1).

Throughout the 1930s (except 1937) the mortality rate in the

62. TsGARK, f. 865, op. 35, sv. 1, d. 4, l. 35.
63. TsGARK, f. 865, op. 35, sv. 1, d. 1, l. 37.

BBLag was lower than the national Gulag average because of the BBLag's importance, its own infrastructure, and the supply routes in existence before the rapid expansion of the penal system. The BBLag mortality rate only exceeded the national average during 1937, and it is possible that this figure includes the significant number of prisoners from the Solovetskii Islands who were executed.

SPECIAL SETTLERS

The effect of special settlers on Karelia was limited because of the presence of the powerful BBLag and the opposition from the Karelian government to yet more "anti-Soviet" elements in the republic. During canal construction, the chairman of the Karelian government, E. Gyulling, managed to redirect thousands of settlers destined for Karelia to Murmansk, where they helped establish a large urban and industrial center at Kirovsk and Apatity.[64] Thousands of settlers were assigned to the BBLag from 1933 onward as the camp and combine were entrusted with the task of creating a permanent population base in the region to provide construction workers for various enterprises. It soon became apparent, however, that local camp administrators were neglecting the settlers and focusing their attention on the camp compounds and on plan fulfillment. Settlers were seen as a drain on local resources since it took several years before they became self-sufficient and began contributing to the combine.[65] Despite orders from the head of BBLag, D. V. Uspenskii, the situation failed to improve; but as the settlers had their civil rights restored, they increasingly became the responsibility of the Karelian authorities, much to the relief of the local Gulag leadership.

---

64. In 1935 there were thirty-five thousand special settlers in the Murmansk region. Between 1931 and 1935, approximately 55–72 percent of the population in this region were settlers. See Joyce, "The Gulag 1930–1960," 161.

65. *Gulag v Karelii, 1930–1941*, doc. No. 92.

CONCLUSION

Before the opening of the Soviet archives, information on the activities of the Gulag in Karelia was largely confined to anecdotal evidence from memoirs and from Gorky's book on the Belomor Canal. None of these sources could give anything more than a glimpse of life in the Karelian Gulag. The official view of life in the Gulag provided by archival evidence has not contradicted the memoir material but has demonstrated the complexity of the Gulag and the constant, conflicting pressures under which it operated. An investigation of the Karelian Gulag has highlighted the experimental nature of forced labor in this region and shown that the practices developed by the BBLag and BBK were soon adopted across the Soviet Union. Up until the mid-1950s, many leading figures in the Gulag spent some part of their careers in Karelia.[66] During the Great Patriotic War, the Gulag was almost completely erased from Karelia, and only a few camps, controlled by the local NKVD, remained in operation. In the postwar world Karelia no longer had a part in determining the future direction of the Soviet Gulag, but it did continue to foreshadow national developments in the application of penal policy.

66. Joyce, "The Gulag 1930–1960," Appendix No. 21.

10 Conclusions

Valery Lazarev

MODERN HISTORY IS characterized by the movement to freedom of labor contract, despite several major setbacks on the way: among them, slavery in the Americas, coolie labor in the Dutch East Indies, and serfdom in Russia. American and Russian forced labor, notably, ended at the same time, in the early 1860s. Some forms of "modern" slavery, especially U.S. slavery, have received considerable attention from economic historians. The more recent experiment with the large-scale use of coerced labor in the Soviet Union received broad literary coverage thanks to the detailed and passionate narratives of survivors, such as Alexander Solzhenitsyn, Evgenia Ginzburg, Varlam Shalamov, and others. There has been, however, little scholarly analysis of the Soviet Gulag as an economic, social, and political institution because of the lack of access to primary data. The decade after the end of the Soviet Union opened even the most secret and painful archives to historians. This book presents the results of years of research by Western and Russian scholars. Some chapters are broad reviews (Chapters 1, 2, and 3); others are case studies of particular "islands" of the "Gulag archipelago."

Coercion in labor relations was fundamental for the Soviet

regime. Introduced as "compulsory labor service" in the first Soviet Constitution of 1918, it remained a legal norm until the end of the USSR. The extent of labor coercion varied over the years, peaking in the heyday of Stalinism, the late 1930s to the early 1950s. Chapter 2 of this volume shows the methods of coercion and the channels through which coerced labor was distributed during this period. These methods included restrictions on the quitting of jobs in all industrial enterprises introduced on the eve of World War II, the conscription-like recruitment of young people into the "labor reserves," and more. The average Soviet workplace was itself a mini-Gulag, where minor infractions carried serious criminal punishments. The most striking development of this period was, however, the rise and fall of the Gulag—the Main Administration for Labor Camps—a system of coerced labor disguised as a penitentiary institution. In fact, the Gulag was a huge "corporation" with hundreds of establishments all over the country, responsible for a significant share of output in such industries as mining, lumber, and construction. The Gulag millions-strong labor force combined hardened criminals with prisoners convicted of imaginary political crimes or of minor felonies related to the infringement of sacrosanct state property—often offenses as petty as stealing a sack of grain.

The brief and brutal history of the Gulag poses several questions. Why did it emerge? Was there an economic rationale for this enterprise or was it the by-product of a selfish dictator's struggle for unchallenged political power? If economic calculation was involved, upon what was it based? The social losses, in the form of high mortality in the Gulag population, are evident. These losses alone do not preclude the possibility that a rational dictator could institute and maintain such a "surplus-extracting" enterprise. However, the dictator's calculation may have been flawed by the distorted economic indicators in his administrative command economy—in stark contrast to slavery in the American South, which was nested in a market economy where a slave-owner could apply market-based economic calculations, treating slaves as capital. In the Soviet Union, the principal miscalculation may have been the notion that Gulag labor was somehow "free," coming at no cost to society.

Although the Gulag's economic significance is obvious, one might see the Gulag merely as a subordinate element in the Stalinist political system. The Gulag began with labor camps, such as the infamous SLON (Solovetskii Camp), which served as an institution for "labor correction." Narratives show that many work assignments in such penal institutions were meaningless and purely punitive. The first notable feat of the Gulag—the White Sea–Baltic Canal—was carried out largely by peasant prisoners who entered the Gulag because of collectivization. The canal opened "on time and on budget" to the drumbeat of publicity by the officious media, but as Khlevnyuk shows in Chapter 3, this project was a waste of resources. The Gulag came into its own with the beginning of the Great Terror in 1937, when the upsurge in political prisoners drastically increased the population of the archipelago. Although the Gulag built and operated such important enterprises as the Magadan gold mines and the Norilsk Nickel Combinat, it could still be argued that the Gulag was primarily an instrument of political persecution. As the morose product of the tyrant's paranoia, its main goal was to accommodate growing numbers of repressed opponents of the regime and "socially alien elements" (like wealthy farmers and priests), while the economic use of prison labor was simply a by-product of the main political purpose.

If this political interpretation of the Gulag is accurate, then the Gulag and Nazi death camps were not essentially different. Both employed their inmates in one way or another, but their ultimate goal was to bury the debris of a never-ending war between the rulers and the population. Although the directors of actual Gulag operations, who had plans to fulfill, understood the importance of the human capital entrusted to them, the dictator did not.

The timeline of the Gulag's history, however, does not support a purely political interpretation of the dictator's intent. Chapter 3 presents the chronology of the Gulag. The first significant step in the institutionalization of coerced labor dates back to the summer of 1929, immediately preceding the mass influx of labor into the camps from the forced collectivization of the peasantry. The first large projects, such as the White Sea–Baltic Canal, Moscow-Volga Canal, and Dalstroi, began in the years 1930–32. Beginning in 1933, the Gulag appears in state investment plans as a separate entity at the same level as an industrial ministry. Collectivization provided for the early growth of the Gulag, but the Gulag grew in importance as an economic unit throughout the 1930s in the absence of further mass political repression campaigns. The Great Terror of 1937 and 1938 increased the number of inmates by about one-half in two short years, but it disrupted Gulag economic operations as much as any other economic enterprises. In Chapter 3, Khlevnyuk suggests that the high number of executions in 1937 and 1938 was caused by the Gulag's inability to accommodate the enormous influx of new inmates. If the Gulag had been only a political penitentiary, its capacity would have been determined by punitive policy and funded accordingly, unrelated to its economic plans. It appears plausible therefore that the Gulag existed autonomously as an economic agent of the government, specializing in the use of prison labor, although political shocks influenced and sometimes overwhelmed its development. The broader picture presented by Sokolov in Chapter 2 shows that the rise of the Gulag fits the general tendency of increasing reliance on coercion in the Stalinist economy after 1937.

The opportunity for the large-scale use of prisoners in locations where free labor did not want to go might seem serendipitous. Archival traces of administrative communications from the period of the first two Five-Year Plans (1928–37) show complaints from enterprise managers in remote areas about the high turnover and problems of recruiting labor. According to Sokolov, attempts to centralize labor contracting through organized recruitment saw little success. In the course of the collectivization campaign that peaked in the period 1929–32, about one million peasant households were ransacked and their members exiled. Collectivization was rational for the selfish dictator since the political benefits (consolidation of power in the countryside) outweighed its economic cost (removal of the most productive farmers to locations where they could not be nearly so productive). Soon collectivization's "unintended benefits" became clear. In 1933, a State Planning Commission (Gosplan) memo on the development of the Far North discussed in a scholarly tone "the recent experience showing that it is beneficial to send sound households to develop remote areas." The analyst, concerned only with the short-run returns for the dictatorial state, naturally did not mention the high percentage of "sound households" that perished in the freezing desert.

The ample evidence presented in this volume suggests that the Stalinist planners and administrators were concerned with the costs and profits of Gulag enterprises—however perverted this notion may be when applied to the ruthless exploitation of prison labor. The evidence also shows that economic calculation (or at least some sort of crude accounting) was used in the evaluation of construction projects that were to receive prison labor input. Obviously, there was no accounting for lost freedom. There was accounting, however, for lost lives—the lost "surplus" from the dictator's point of view—except in periods when the overwhelming increases in the number of prisoners created the perception of endless pools of costless labor. In periods of relative stability, the Gulag administration was concerned with the mortality and morbidity rates of the prison population, a natural concern of a selfish ruler who has a sufficiently long time horizon, but not of a tyrant who seeks only to destroy his political enemies.

Gulag economic calculation was distorted, as in other parts of the economy, by administrated prices. In particular, the Gulag had no notion of capital markets that would have allowed for the cynical but accurate valuation of inmate-capital in the same way as slaves. The Gulag accounting did not go beyond the short run, focusing on inmate subsistence and the personnel payroll. A large part of the fixed cost of coercion fell below the Gulag's radar screen. In fact, coercion was expensive, and its cost was not limited to the payment of camp guards. Coercion required the creation of a legal and technical infrastructure that could not be internalized by a single labor camp or even the entire Gulag. Major Gulag camps were located far from inhabited areas: in Siberia, the European North, and Kazakhstan. Narratives show that Kolyma prisoners, assigned to a new job, often hiked from one camp to another without convoy. There was no way to escape. The concentration of forced labor was particularly beneficial when the natural environment itself lowered security costs or even created increasing returns to the investment in security. Moreover, as Chapter 5 shows, nominally free workers in isolated locations like Norilsk could be treated in much the same way as prisoners. At the same time, hiring out prisoners to civil enterprises created security costs. Therefore, the geography of the Gulag may have been not only the result of the wish to launch projects in areas where free labor was prohibitively expensive but also of the constraints on coercion expenditures.

To place prisoners in locations where the cost of coercion was low, the Gulag had to bear the high cost of transporting them to remote locations. Furthermore, the benefit of the low cost of coercion in isolated locations contradicted the goals of development. Better roads that lowered transportation costs also broke the isolation and increased the probability of escapes. There were additional hidden costs of coercion. Not only the camp guards and harsh Siberian terrain coerced prisoners; in effect, the whole country was a single police network. Maintaining this network was not the Gulag's responsibility, but Gulag leaders were its beneficiaries. The

Gulag was in a sense a free-rider on the huge machinery of coercion run by Stalin's government.

Gulag special interests deserve particular mention. As an economic agency of the state, the Gulag was given a certain autonomy, was subject to budget constraints (although soft, as in other Soviet economic units), and was rewarded when successful in fulfilling its plans. As a producer, it sought to obtain the optimal mix of labor skills to execute its projects. Therefore it had to resort to hiring free, qualified labor. On the other hand, the Gulag was given the monopoly right for distributing "costless" prison labor, as Chapter 1 points out. The Gulag naturally sought to clear the balance by hiring out excess prison labor to civil enterprises. The fact that it secured the right to contract out labor is remarkable, given the generally negative attitude in the Soviet economy toward any form of lease. It was thought that resources should be allocated optimally; if an agency could not use its resources it should yield them back to the state rather than rent them out. Since the Gulag received revenue from leasing prison labor, the possibility existed that the Gulag might turn into a rent-seeker, fighting for increases in the prison population for the sole purpose of hiring out prisoners. The figures in Table 1.3 in Chapter 1 suggest that the process was under way—the share of "contract workers" increased from 11 percent in 1941 to 25 percent in 1950—and was restrained only in the last years of the Gulag's existence.

The main hidden cost of coercion is the loss of productivity. To induce workers to exert more effort, a manager can choose to increase wages, supervision, or supervision in its extreme form, coercion. Low pay alone may not be the best solution if the productivity of penal labor is sufficiently lower than that of free labor. If penal workers are paid 50 percent less but are 50 percent less productive, the cost of labor per unit of output is the same. If the wages of free workers are 50 percent above subsistence and penal workers are paid at subsistence, free labor is "cheaper" if the productivity of free workers is more than 50 percent higher than that of penal labor. The decisive turn toward coercion in the 1930s thus signals that the Stalinist leadership, "dizzy with success" over collectivization, came to believe that penal workers, like collectivized peasants, could be forced to work efficiently without real material incentives. Chapters 2 and 5 show that by the late 1940s Gulag administrators realized the inefficiency of coercion combined with low pay. They started introducing material incentives in labor camps, thus closing the gap between free and prison labor.

And what about the "benefits" of the Gulag? The argument that forced labor created projects of high value for the national economy, such as the Norilsk Combinat, which produces today a substantial share of the world's output of platinum and nickel, does not disprove the existence of better alternatives. Free workers avoided going to the Far North, not because of an idiosyncratic aversion to its harsh climate, but because they were never offered adequate compensation. If the enterprise promised such high returns, it would have been rational to pay wages high enough to attract highly productive free labor. Instead the government used its resources to amass overwhelming coercive power to force inmates to work at subsistence wages, thus reducing accounting cost in the short run.

It is easy to misjudge the Gulag's contribution because its more lasting monuments—the Moscow metro, the Moscow University, and the Norilsk Nickel Combinat—are what remain. Forgotten are the "roads to nowhere," long fallen into the decay that is not unique to Gulag projects. The countries of the former Soviet Union are cemeteries of failed construction projects, which would never have been started if project analysis had not been distorted by the absence of market pricing in the national economy and by the country's isolation from international markets. Many such projects came into being merely because of fleeting political considerations.

The end of the Gulag can be regarded as a declaration of bankruptcy in the strict economic sense. In the early 1950s, it found itself unprofitable: its revenues were not sufficient to cover the cost of its active labor force and the maintenance of the nonworking part of the Gulag population. The Gulag had to plead for subsidies from the state budget. Gulag managers were aware that the labor productivity of its workers was 50 to 60 percent lower than that of free workers. Near its end, the Gulag employed one guard for every ten workers. It is noteworthy that it was Lavrenty Beria, the head of the secret police and the ultimate Gulag insider, who argued in favor of shutting down the system. Beria, probably better than others, understood the Gulag's deep economic flaws. The cynical logic of the rising dictatorship brought the Gulag into being, and the pragmatism of the post-Stalinist regime put it to an end.

List of Acronyms

AOPDFRK	Archive of Socio-Political Movements and Formations of the Republic of Karelia
BAM	Baikal-Amur Mainline
BAMLag	Baikal-Amur Camp
BBK	White Sea–Baltic Combine
BBLag	White Sea–Baltic Camp
CPSU	Communist Party of the Soviet Union
Dalstroi	Far North Construction Trust
GAMO	State Archive of the Magadan Region
GARF	State Archive of Russian Federation
Glavk (pl. glavki)	Main Economic Administration
Glavpromstroi	Main Administration of Industrial Construction
Gosbank	State Bank
Gosplan	State Planning Commission
GUGidroStroi	Main Administration of Hydraulic Construction
Gulag	Main Administration of Camps
GULGMP	Main Administration of Camps in Mining and Metallurgy Industry

GULLP	Administration of Camps in Forestry and Wood Processing
GULPS	Main Administration of Camps for Industrial Construction
GULSchosDor	Main Administration of Camps for Highway Construction
GULZhDS	Chief Camp Administration of Railway Construction
GUShDS	Main Administration of Railroad Construction
GUShosDor	Main Administration of Roadway Construction
ITL	Corrective Labor Camp
KVO	Cultural-Educative Department
MGB	Ministry of State Security
MVD	Ministry of Internal Affairs
Narkomtrud	People's Commissariat (Ministry) of Labor
Narkomvnudel	See NKVD
NEP	New Economic Policy
NKVD	People's Commissariat (Ministry) of Internal Affairs
Norillag	Norilsk Labor Camp
Norilstroi	Norilsk Construction Administration
Politburo	Supreme Body of CPSU
OGPU	United State Political Administration (secret police in 1923–1934)
RGAE	Russian State Archive of the Economy
RGASPI	Russian State Archive of Social and Political History
SLON (also SLAG)	Solovetskii Camp of Special Significance
Sevvostlag	Northeastern Camps
SNK (also Sovnarkom)	Council of People's Commissars (government)

STO	Council of Labor and Defense (a commission of SNK)
TsGARK	Central State Archive of the Republic of Karelia
TsKhSDMO	Center for the Preservation of the Modern Documents of the Magadan Region
ULLP	Administration of Camps in Forestry and Wood Processing
ULTP	Administration of Camps in Heavy Industry
USiKMITL	Administration of Camps Solovetskii and Karelo-Murmansk Corrective-Labor
URO	Department of Records and Assignments of the Gulag
USLON	Administrative of Northern Camps of Special Significance
USSR	Union of Soviet Socialist Republics

Index

White Sea–Baltic Camp (*continued*)
169; living conditions at, 184–85;
mortality rate at, 185–86; security
at, 180–81; settlers for, 186; under
Timofeev, 174–76
White Sea–Baltic (Belomor) Canal
(BBK), Belomor administration of,
156; budget for, 153–54, 156–57,
161, 166; completion of, ix, 46,
151, 161, 167; construction of, 39,
61, 133, 152, 156; equipment for,
156–60; executions at, 175;
incentives for, 160–61; labor for,
155, 158, 159–61, 166; military use
of, 161–62; norms for, 160–61;
organizational methods for, 46;
plans for, 3, 155, 159; value of, 62,
161
White Sea–Baltic (Belomor) Canal,
Administration of, 156
White Sea–Baltic (Belomor) Combine.
See White Sea–Baltic (Belomor)
Canal
Winter War, 178, 184
work brigade, 90–91, 160
work credit, system of, 40, 49–51, 55,
92–95, 120–21, 161
work effort, measurement of, 85
work hours, 88–89
work norms, 90, 142, 148, 150
work refusal, 24, 65, 90, 92, 161
work transfer, 91. *See also* incentives,
Gulag

working conditions, 33–34
workplace coercion, 6, 24–26, 30, 42,
150, 192
World War II, aftermath of, 32–39;
destruction by, 32; female labor
during, 29–30; Finnish/Soviet
border during, 177; mobilization
for, 30, 36; Nazi invasion of, 25,
50; patriotism during, 29, 39;
prisoner reduction by, 11, 39, 50–
51, 78, 148–49, 190; production
during, 29; service in, 84
wreckers, 113

Yagoda, G. G., 1; as Gulag architect,
68, 170; Norilsk plans by, 133–34;
productivity under, 183; White Sea–
Baltic (Belomor) Canal, 154, 158,
166–67
Yenisei Steam Navigation Company,
130
Yezhov, N. I., 1–2, 118, 170
Yezhovschina, 118. *See also* Great
Purges
young pioneers, 27

Zaveniagin, A. P., 141–43. *See also*
Norillag
Zavenyagin, S., 84, 87
zek (Gulag prisoner), 2, 120. *See also*
prisoners, Gulag; specialists
Zverev, V. S., 83, 93, 94